Contents

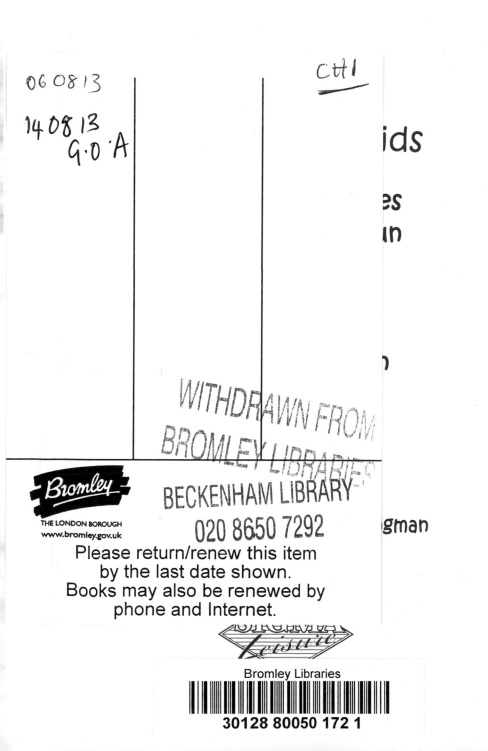

© Angela Youngman, 2011

All Rights Reserved. No part of this publication may be reproduced, stored in a retrieval system, or transmitted in any form or by any means – electronic, mechanical, photocopying, recording, or otherwise – without prior written permission from the publisher

Published by Sigma Leisure – an imprint of
Sigma Press, Stobart House, Pontyclerc, Penybanc Road
Ammanford, Carmarthenshire SA18 3HP

British Library Cataloguing in Publication Data

A CIP record for this book is available from the British Library

ISBN: 978-1-85058-887-0

Typesetting and Design by: Sigma Press, Ammanford, Carms

Drawings: © Karis Youngman

Cover drawing: © Karis Youngman

Printed by: Berforts Group Ltd

Introduction

Walking with kids can be fun or a nightmare depending on how you choose to approach it. Just saying "we are going for a walk" and expecting children to walk several miles is a sure fire way of attracting protests, complaints and unhappy children. All parents are accustomed to the constant query "How much further?" and "I'm tired, I want to go home." Yet, with just a little bit of thought and preparation, this situation can be avoided. By keeping children occupied and interested, they will walk much further than they think they can.

Going for a walk needs to be approached the right way. It is not just a matter of saying "we are going for a walk" and expecting kids to walk several miles. Children are not interested in the idea of walking for the sake of walking. An adult will quite happily go for a walk – a child needs a reason to go. Walking for exercise is not a strong enough reason for kids, especially if you are hoping to have a walk that lasts longer than five or ten minutes.

Children like to have reasons and things to do when they go for a walk. Telling them they are going for a walk results in immediate objections especially if it is cold or they are busy doing something within the house. However, if you approach the activity from the point of view of going for a walk to play Green Man in the woods, hunt for minibeasts, play Hobbits or track animal trails – children react very differently. Coats and shoes are sought out and they will happily go out for an hour or more.

Never say how far you plan to walk – even half a mile sounds a long way. Stating the length of a walk before you start usually acts as a deterrent. Instead, say you are going to a wood, or for a scramble along the sand dunes, to explore Robin Hood's forest or the land where King Arthur ruled – this will have much more impact and children's attention will be caught. Look too for unusual themed walks. Many places have guided walks based on themes such as local history or nature. There may be sculpture or Green Man trails available. Again, such activities add interest to the walk and help keep a child's attention.

Make sure that children are suitably dressed. Being cold and wet will not encourage to them to walk very far. Wearing rubber boots for splashing through puddles, and having extra jerseys and waterproofs when necessary makes a lot of difference. Have a small first aid kit at hand – scratches and grazes are all too common.

It also helps to have something to look forward to at the end of a walk. A hot drink, an ice cream, a special activity or a meal can make all the difference especially when tiredness begins to set in.

When they are having fun, children will walk further than they think they can. The length of the walk becomes less of an issue because they are concentrating on what is happening around them.

However, always make sure that the eventual walk length is suitable to a child's age and ability. Be realistic. An adult may easily walk seven, ten or more miles – a child would find this difficult to achieve. Never try to do too much. Remember children do have shorter legs and do get tired more quickly. No matter how many activities you provide, you will not get children to walk several miles without getting used to the idea of walking some distance. Giving children a break at regular intervals will encourage them to go a bit further. Increase the length of your walks slowly and gradually.

When planning a walk, get children involved from the beginning. Let them look at maps and help decide on routes. Introduce as much variety as possible into the various walks you plan – try and include different habitats and different environments. This will encourage them to walk further since it is a route they have chosen rather than having it imposed on them. Older children could practise map reading as they walk.

Take some friends with you. When children are talking to their friends and playing with them, they do not realise just how far they have walked. It adds to the fun and encourages them to go just that bit further.

This book aims to provide lots of ideas and suggestions for activities, games and things to do while walking. From well-known favourites like Hide and Seek and I spy to Mouse, Find the Alien, environmental art, and foraging – there is something for everyone. There are games for groups of children, and games suitable for just one or two. Spread out the activities so that they occur at different points in the walk. Vary them as much as possible – this adds extra interest for the children.

To be effective, you need to organise your walk making sure that you have any equipment such as scarves, paper, or containers that are needed to complete a particular activity. Choose a range of activities and games to suit the location and the weather conditions as well as the length of walk you are planning. Keep it varied as this will help keep children interested.

Out for a walk

Country code

- Dress sensibly – remember that in all but the driest times, paths through woodlands or along steams can be wet and muddy. Sturdy shoes or rubber boots are required

- If on mountains or moors, mists can appear quickly and temperatures fall. Having warm, waterproof clothing available is essential

- Always take home all the equipment and materials you have brought with you. Leave nothing behind

- Do nothing to harm the environment

- Do not break down trees

- Do not swing from branches – they might break and children can get hurt

- Do nothing to harm wildlife

- Do not disturb nesting birds

- Leave no litter

- Do not allow children or dogs to chase wildlife or grazing animals

- Do not cut branches without permission

- Always consider the needs of other users of the countryside. If people are sitting quietly on a seat, they may not want children screaming beside them

- Choose sites for games where they will not annoy other users of the countryside

- Do not trespass on private property

- Stay on public pathways, marked paths and countryside open to the public

- If you light a fire, make sure that it is fully out before leaving the area

- If you open gates, always make sure they are closed when you have passed through

- Keep dogs under control and on a lead when walking through fields full of animals

Safety notes

- Accidents can happen so it is important to be prepared

- Take a small first aid kit with you – scratches, scrapes and cuts are all too common and it is better to deal with them immediately rather than risking any chance of infection

- When playing games like hide and seek, clearly identifying the boundaries beyond which children should not go is important. Put something noticeable such as a brightly coloured jersey or raincoat in a prominent position like on a tree branch to decrease the chances of anyone getting lost. Make sure that children always know they should go to that spot if worried or lost

- Carry a whistle and ensure that children know they must always return to you immediately if they hear it

- Children should not talk to strangers

- Children should never go too far from the rest of the group and should not wander off alone

- Before starting a game such as Camouflage or Tracking; make sure everyone knows where the meeting point is located, and where they must return immediately they hear the whistle

- Do not eat wild foods unless an adult has given permission

- Do not allow children to play unsupervised near water of any kind

Games

Playing games are always fun and guaranteed to keep kids motivated. It can provide learning opportunities too, but these should never be stressed as it can turn kids off the whole idea of going for a walk. A brief explanation about why birds need to find food, why rubbish should not be left in the wild or how animals can be tracked through the woods is all that is required.

Some of the games may need a little preparation before you leave home, for example you may need to collect up items such as scarves. Many of the games will need nothing more than what you can find en route.

The amount of time taken to play a game will depend entirely on the children involved. Sometimes it may be just a few minutes, other times allow at least 15 to 30 minutes.

Bat and moth

Take: Scarves

This game is most effective played at night when moths and bats are around, but can be played anytime. You need a clear space in which to play. Several children or adults are needed.

To play the game, one child has to be blindfolded using a scarf and becomes the bat. Another child is the moth. All other players stand in a ring around them, arms outstretched to ensure the moth and bat do not escape the ring. The bat has to catch the moth. This is done by calling out "Where are you?" The bat has to listen hard for the answer "here". The moth has to answer each time the bat calls. The bat has to move in the direction of the sound and try and catch the moth. The moth can move around, and has to try to evade being caught. All the other players keep very quiet and provide no help to either moth or bat. When the bat has caught the moth, other children can have a turn.

Why not make it more complicated by having two moths in the circle at any one time!

Bat on the hunt

This game seeks to mirror the way in which bats catch their prey. They listen constantly for movement.

Bear Hunt

Perfect for younger children, who enjoy the story and variety of movement. Based around the Bear Hunt song you make up different types of movement to suit the environment you are walking through.

The song begins "We're going on a bear hunt! We're gonna catch a big one! I'm not afraid!"

There are numerous verses all in the same style such as "We're coming to a tall mountain. It sure is high. It sure is wide. Let's climb up it. Well, there's nothing over there. Hey wait, I think I see something. Quick, everybody run down!"

Or "We're coming to a patch of grass, tall wavy grass. We can't go over it, we can't go under it, we'll have to go through it! Swish, swish, swish."

A mountain setting could be taken to be a hill, a mound, even just climbing over a log at the side of the path. Other typical scenes could include "We're going through pine needles", "We're going through a patch of mud", "We're going over a bridge", "We're going through a puddle, splash, splash, splash"

Encourage the child to use their imagination to come up with suitable words to describe actions and build these into the story, along with any other activities that they want to include.

Eventually it ends with the child finding a bear – perhaps by looking into the undergrowth near the path then running away.

Blindfold Walking

Take: Scarves to use as blindfolds

The aim is to see what can be identified without using your eyes. It helps to develop other senses such as hearing and touch.

Blindfold the child, and then lead them for a short distance along the path. As they walk, encourage them to feel trees, leaves, rocks, put their hands in a rock pool or listen to a bird singing. Collect wild herbs and scented leaves and see if the child can guess what they are. If different surfaces such as a muddy puddle, a stony path or sandy surface are available, take the blindfolded child over them and see if they can work out what they are treading on. After they have made a guess as to the identity of an object, then tell them what it is.

Bird and hawk

Take: Something for each bird to sit on. This could be carpet tiles, or a large branch, or piece of newspaper – these are the nests. Small sticks/straws or pieces of dried spaghetti

This is a game for a large group of children. Adults can join in too if they want. To be really effective, at least eight participants are needed. It can be played at any point during a walk. It is a variation on musical chairs but with a nature theme.

Choose one child to be the hawk. All the others are birds. Place the nests in a rough circle. Put the small sticks some distance away in two or three locations. The aim is for the 'birds' to dash from their nests, grab a piece of food and get back to their nest without being caught by the roving hawk. All birds caught turn into additional hawks.

The task is made harder as one nest is removed each time the birds make a run for food. The birds have to compete for nests. Anyone who cannot find a nest becomes a hawk. Who is the last bird to survive?

Kestrel

Camouflage Hide and Seek

This is a variant on the traditional game of hide and seek. One person is the seeker; the other people are the hiders. The aim is to avoid being found for as long as possible. However, unlike traditional hide and seek, those hiding have to use camouflage rather than hiding behind something. They need to blend in with their surroundings and stay as still as possible.

This is most effective if the children are wearing muted colours – a brightly coloured T-shirt can quickly give a child's location away!

Choose a stretch of path for the game. Everyone should know the limits of the area in which they can hide. Encourage the children to hide close to the path, blending in as far as possible with their surroundings. The seeker should walk along the path looking for those in hiding. If the seeker passes them, the hiders can jump up victorious since the seeker had not been able to see through their camouflage.

This is a game that can be played on the move, while you are walking. Just give the children long enough to hide a short distance ahead.

When they are found or are victorious over you (the seeker), they can try again a bit further on along the path.

Camouflage Capture

This is most effective with larger groups of children ideally at least six participants.

Play the game in a clearing or area where there are lots of shrubs and bushes, which can be used as camouflage. Divide the children into two teams. Each team should be given a base. The task is to capture the other team's base without being caught. To do so, they have to move stealthily through the countryside, taking advantage of any natural features so as to blend into the background.

Encourage children to move carefully when they are playing this game. They should:

- Move quietly without any sudden movements
- Crouch down and crawl on their stomachs
- When standing they should hide behind trees or large bushes and make sure their silhouettes do not break the skyline
- Use natural features such as trees and hollows as hiding places
- Keep to the shadows
- When moving or standing still, adopt shapes which reflect surrounding natural features such as bushes or boulders
- Be patient and take their time!

There are variants on this game:

One child could be left in each base to watch for other children creeping through the countryside. If seen, they have to go back to their own base and start again.

One child guards a central point. All the other children have to try and creep up and capture it.

This is a game that can take some time. It cannot be hurried. The slower and more carefully the children move, the less likely it is that they will be noticed. Children whose clothes blend into the countryside, such as wearing lots of green, brown or khaki will also have an advantage.

Making camouflage clothing by adding lots of leaves to their hair or tucked into their clothing may help. Alternatively they can make a netting cloak (see under Netting Cloaks in chapter 3). Using face paints can help disguise the shape and colour of the face.

Collections

Take : Scarves

While walking look for interesting objects which have varying textures and shapes such as feathers, acorns, conkers, pieces of moss or shells. When several items have been collected, have a short break. Fasten a scarf as a blindfold round the child's eyes, and let them feel the various items. Can they identify what the item is by touch alone?

To make it more complex when several children are present, children keep their collections secret. The blindfolded child is given the unknown objects found by another child and has to guess what they are.

Explorers

Any number of children can be involved. Divide into two groups – explorers and monsters. Monsters go ahead and find places to jump out and try to catch the 'explorers' unawares. The explorers walk on along the path and pretend to be explorers in an undiscovered country. All kinds of strange things might be found as you walk through the woods or fields – there might also be monsters waiting to grab you. Try and create an atmosphere as you walk by asking questions in low voices such as "What's that over there?" "Was that something grey hiding in the bushes?" "Where will the monsters be?" "Can you avoid being caught by them?"

Find the Alien

Any number of children can play this game. It can be played as you walk along a path, in a clearing or simply choosing an area and letting children investigate it thoroughly. It makes children look more closely at their environment and the effects of litter.

The aim is to find things that should not be there particularly alien, man made objects that do not fit into the environment. Look for items of litter such as crisp packets, sweet wrappers, cans, bottles, bits of wool, plastic bags and other man made objects. If you have more than one child playing the game, it can be turned into a competitive activity. Who can find the most alien objects?

Asking the children to work out why these items should not be there could extend this activity. What are

Unwanted rubbish

the dangers to animals? An empty bottle for example might attract a mouse – but once in, the smooth sides prevent them from climbing out again. As a result the mouse dies of starvation. A smelly crisp packet can attract a hungry animal. Thinking it is food; they often try to eat it. This can make them ill and possibly even kill them. Pieces of glass can cut paws or hands. It can also cause fires in certain conditions. Plastic will not degrade.

At the end of the game, why not be a good environmentalist and put all the rubbish you have found into a bag for disposal in the nearest rubbish bin?

Flags

Take : Two flags

This is a game that can be played in a clearing or at a convenient break time during a walk. Look for an area where there is some cover from bushes and shrubs. Divide the children into two teams. Each team chooses a place to put their flag. The aim is to capture the other team's flag without being seen. Children have to creep from bush to bush, wriggling along the ground, move carefully and quietly. One person should be left with each flag to guard it. If they see anyone, they have to call out that person's name. If spotted that person has to return to their home flag and start again. An adult should act as a referee – otherwise the arguments can get rather loud!

Grandmother's footsteps

This is a variant on the traditional game of What's the Time Mr Wolf? It is also sometimes known as Statues. It can be played anywhere along the walk, and can take as long or as little time as you like.

To play the game, one person should be allotted the title of Grandmother. The rest of the players spread out in a row some distance behind her. The aim is to sneak up very quietly behind 'Grandmother' and tap on the shoulder. The task is made harder by the fact that 'Grandmother' can turn round at any point. Everyone has to stop and immediately become a statue holding the position they were in when 'Grandmother' turned round. If she sees you move, then you have to go back to the start point.

Green man arise

Find – Lots of dry leaves

This is a game best played with at least four or more children. Choose a dry day in the autumn when the leaves have been falling quite thickly onto the ground. Look for a dry area that has a thick covering of leaves and no sharp branches, brambles or nettles nearby. Check the leaves to make sure there is no rubbish or pieces of glass hidden underneath.

To play the game, one child has to be chosen to be the 'green man' or 'green woman'. The child lies on the ground and is totally covered with leaves. All the other children gather around in a rough circle and chant the words "Green Man arise. Green Man Arise." If a girl has been buried, alter the words to "Green Woman Arise, Green Woman Arise". The words are chanted continuously until the 'Green Man' suddenly jumps up, scattering leaves around and chases the other children. If a child is caught, then that child becomes the next 'Green Man'. If no child is caught, the Green Man lies down and is reburied in the leaves and the chant begins again.

This is a game that can take quite a long time to play, as every child wants to have at least one turn. It is a fun game that can be played by all ages.

Hide and Seek

One of the oldest and most popular of games and has wide spread appeal with all ages. It can be played with any number of children and adults. Hide and Seek can be played anywhere there is some potential hiding places available even if it is just behind trees or shrubs.

The rules are simple – one person is the seeker and has the task of finding everyone else. The seeker closes his/her eyes and turns away from the rest of the group before counting to an agreed number (usually 100). Everyone else scatters and finds places to hide. When the seeker has finished counting he/she calls "coming ready or not"; turns round and starts to search for people. When everyone is found, someone else should take a turn as seeker.

The length of the game can vary. It depends on how many people play, how many want to be seekers and how easy it is to find everyone.

When playing this game, make sure that everyone knows the boundaries of the area they can use for hiding. No one, especially young children, should go outside that area. Place a brightly coloured jersey or coat at a central point, to provide a meeting point if anyone gets lost. It will provide something to aim for which is easy to see.

Hobbits

Divide into two groups. The smaller group are the Black Riders. The larger group are Hobbits on the way to Mordor. They have to avoid the deadly Black Riders who may appear at any moment. Will they catch you? Can you spot them in the distance and hide before they find you? This is a fun game that can be played as you walk along a path.

Hop skip and jump

Explore different ways of moving as you walk. Bored with walking, try hopping, jumping or skipping along. Take a skipping rope and

skipping

see how far the child can skip. What about walking on tip toe so as not to frighten the animals and birds or trying to walk as quietly as possible without making a sound or breaking a twig? When walking across a field or common full of molehills, try jumping over the molehills. It is surprising how far children will go when asked to vary the way they walk!

Ice games

Make sure that the ice is safe to stand on. Do not try to play games on pools, rivers or lakes, as this rarely freezes hard enough to bear your weight.

Look for patches of ice on thinly flooded fields, or large even large puddles.

There are many games that can be played:

Ice Hockey
Use sticks to manoeuvre a small stone across the ice. This is particularly suitable for several children working in teams. One side of the iced area marks the goal posts for one team, the other side for the second team. Who can score the most goals? Great care has to be taken not to break the ice!

Ice skittles
For this you need some smaller pieces of ice and a small heap of stones. Pile the stones at one end of the ice area, then slide pieces of ice across to see if you can knock down the stone pile.

Ice curling

Slide smaller pieces of ice across the surface. Whose ice piece will go the furthest?

Ice jumping

As you walk, look for patches of ice. Jump on them and break them into small pieces. Listen to the sounds of the cracking ice. Whose cracks are the loudest?

Islands

Look for an area where there are several tree stumps in a row. Alternatively lay out some large leaves such as horse chestnut leaves in a series of circles. The circles should not be touching. The object is to jump from one to another without touching the ground between them. If you touch the ground between the circles, then you can be caught by sharks (the other children).

Know a tree

Take: Scarves to use as blindfolds

Choose an area where there are no fallen down trees, patches of nettle or bramble. A clearing surrounded by trees is ideal. Children need to be able to get close to the trees and to touch all parts of the trunk safely. When choosing a tree make sure there are no outstretched branches into which the children can walk when trying to identify 'their' tree.

Divide children into pairs or one adult and a child. Use the scarf to blindfold the child. Then turn the blindfolded child round several times so that they lose their sense of direction. Carefully guide the child towards a tree ensuring they do not trip up or walk into anything. If you have to divert from a straight line do not tell them why – just let them sense they are moving slightly to the right or left. When the tree is reached, put the child's hands onto the bark.

The blindfolded child has to move around the tree, exploring all aspects of it, finding out what it feels like and trying to identify by feel any lumps or bumps in the trunk. Encourage them to think about what it smells like. Think about what size it is by trying to put their arms around it. Feel the ground around it – is it mossy, dry leaves, roots sticking out? Give them a few minutes to do this.

Then, take the blindfolded child by the hand and move back to the starting position. Take off the blindfold. Their task is to try and find 'their' tree, using only their memory of the journey and their senses of touch and smell. When they succeed, (or give up!) the other person in the pair is blindfolded and led to a different tree that they then have to try and identify.

This is a game that generally leads to a lot of laughter, especially when trying to find a tree after being blindfolded. The amount of time this game takes depends entirely on the number of children involved and the number of times they want to play it.

It helps develop a sense of touch, smell and confidence.

Listening games

Ask the children to sit or lie down, separate from each other. They have to be very, very quiet and listen hard. What can they hear?

Set a time limit. When the time is up, each child sits up where they are and tells everyone what they have heard. A competitive element can be introduced – who has heard the most? An adult will be needed to act as referee to make sure that nothing is made up to swell the numbers.

Variations on this activity include:

- Can anyone identify ten natural sounds?
- What sounds can they hear that do not belong in the natural environment?
- How many bird calls they can identify?

Try this game in different habitats – in a wood, in a meadow, by a lake. What differences can be found?

The biggest range of sounds can be heard in the early morning or at dusk.

Memory

Find – A collection of natural items such as a feather, oak leaf, pine cone, acorn, moss, sticks

Show collection to the children. Give them say one minute to memorise the items. Put the collection away. Their task is to try to find an example of everything they saw simply by relying on their memory. Can they remember what they saw? It is a good memory test as well as a good memory training activity for everyone – adults included!

Mouse

Take: A small plastic bottle with a tightly fitting lid for each person taking part, hot water, red food colouring to represent blood

This game looks at how animals hibernate and the dangers it can present. It is best played at the beginning of a walk that starts and ends in the same place. It can be played many times always with different endings since some locations will be more successful than others.

mouse

Begin by fixing a label to each bottle so that every child can easily identify 'their' bottle. Fill each bottle with hot water and add a few drops of red food colouring. Tighten the lid securely. This is your 'mouse', which needs to survive the winter. Find a warm place in which the 'mouse' can hibernate. This might be under a pile of leaves, under a bush, in the trunk of a tree. Put the 'mouse' in place and cover it up. Leave it there while you go for a walk.

When you return to the spot, each child has to find their 'mouse'. Is the water still warm? If so, your 'mouse' has survived the winter. If the water is cold, then the 'mouse' will have died.

Ask children: How could the 'mouse' have been better protected? Did it need a deeper leaf covering? What could you do better next time?

Password

Take – Scarves for blindfolds

Any number of children can play. This is a game for playing in a clearing or in a field. One person needs to be the referee. Divide into two groups. One group should be larger than the other. Blindfold each member of the smaller group. They are the explorers. The explorers should choose a password such as Oak or Ash. The larger group should spread out around them and stand very still. Each person in the larger group should pretend to be an animal or tree and make quiet noises reminiscent of the animal or tree. For example, a tree might sway in the wind, or a mouse might squeak. The explorers have to listen carefully and try to make their way through the 'forest' without hitting any of the obstacles in their path. If explorers bump into each other they should whisper the password. The person who is first through all the obstacles to the other side is the winner.

This game can be made more difficult and longer. One member of the larger group should be named Wolf. No one makes a sound unless an explorer touches him or her. But if an explorer touches the Wolf, he roars and all the explorers have to return to their original starting point and re-start the game.

Pixie potions

Take - Small container
Find – A stick for mixing

This game will appeal to younger children. It is also a way of helping them to understand that eating the wrong sort of plants can make them ill.

Make up a short story line such as: One day, little pixie woke up feeling ill. Her tummy hurt and she did not want to get out of bed. "I shouldn't have eaten those berries yester-day" she said. Her mother had the answer. "What you need is a potion, something to make you feel better." The children's job is to make up that potion by collecting items either around them, or on the walk. Ask what they think would make the pixie feel better? Should it be sweet smelling or smell nasty? Should it be a mix of colours, or just one colour? What would work best?

Rather than drinking the potion, the pixie will get better or worse by smelling it.

As they choose, explain that some plants will make people ill and that berries and fungi

Little pixie

should not be touched, picked or eaten unless you know they are harmless. Bright red toadstools or berries may look pretty – but they can make you ill. Such things should be avoided in the pixie potion because they will make little pixie feel even worse. Mix the ingredients together with a stick at regular intervals to release the aroma.

Robin Hood

At the end of the game, empty the container and take it home.

Robin Hood

This is best played with a group of children, ideally at least six. Smaller numbers may mean adults are needed to join in! Everyone knows the stories of Robin Hood and his Merrie Men at war with the Sheriff of Nottingham. Divide into two groups – Robin Hood and his band of outlaws, and the Sheriff of Nottingham and his men. Try acting out a scene such as the sheriff capturing Maid Marian and Robin rescuing her. This is ideal for a clearing or the edge of woodland.

You could also play an ambush style game. Robin Hood and his men have to ambush you as you walk along the path. But beware – the secret to success is careful ambushing and being very quiet. Giggling and rustling may lead to discovery – in which they lose and have to try again elsewhere.

Rope trails

Take – One rope, scarves to use as blindfolds

Blindfold rope trail

This is most fun if played with several children. There are variations to the game, depending on where you are playing it.

On a hill – lay a rope down the hillside avoiding any major obstacles. An adult should stand at the top anchoring the rope in place. Children run to the bottom of the hill and put on blindfolds. They are taken to the rope and then use it haul themselves to the top of the hill, all the time trying to work out what they walking over or through.

Fixed rope trail in a clearing. Tie the rope to a tree then lay it out so that children hold it at hand height. Depending on the age of the children incorporate various obstacles such as gaps through bushes, walking on a log, or crawling through a bush. Tie the other end of the rope to another tree. Children put on blindfolds then try to navigate the course by touch, using the rope for guidance. Younger children may need some help.

Blindfold walk

This can take the form of a moving trail along the path. One adult is needed at the front of the rope, another at the end. Children are blindfolded and placed at intervals along the rope. The adult leads the way, warning the children about any obstacles they may encounter. When playing this game, it is important to keep the rope taut.

Afterwards, encourage the children to think about what it was like finding their way around blindfolded and unable to see. How did it feel? What were the problems?

Safari

This is ideal for playing in a meadow or area of long grass with younger children. It can even be played as you walk along providing there is scope for the children to move stealthily through the grass nearby. One person is the spotter and the others are 'animals'. As they attempt to move along unnoticed through the grass, the 'animals' have to make appropriate sounds to match their character, eg: a donkey braying, or a horse neighing. The spotter's task is to find each 'animal', identifying the animal and exactly where they are in the area.

Scavenger hunts

Take – A bag for each child to use when collecting their finds

Scavenger hunts are great fun. It gives children a reason for walking and can be undertaken in almost any environment. Their task is to collect up items to match a list, letter or colour. So for example, younger children could be asked to go for a walk collecting examples of items which are brown, or to search for different leaves. Older children could be given a list of items to be found such as something unusual, something white and fluffy, something green, something non-organic, something spiky, something found on birds, a seed that catches a lift, something that protects a plant.

To succeed in the scavenger hunt, children have to be observant, and to look closely at their environment.

Once they get used to the idea you can theme the scavenger hunts or make them longer and more complex. The amount of preparation needed beforehand depends entirely on how complex you want to make it. Potential topics for scavenger hunts can include:

- Different types of feathers
- Things beginning with a specific letter of the alphabet
- Unusual items – and the children have to explain why they are unusual
- Items relating to food
- Seeds
- Spiky items
- Soft items
- Grass seed heads

Miniature scavenging

Give each child a very small container such as a matchbox. Their task is to find items which would fit into the box. They may have to find a set number of items, or to simply see how many things they can fit inside. Typical items can include a seed, a pine needle, a small stone, and a thorn.

Puzzled by the list!

Impossible scavenging

This can be really challenging. Give children a list of items that they have to find – but are impossible to physically collect for example an oak tree, a squirrel's drey or a rabbit hole. When they find it, they have to show it to you before it can be marked off the list.

Set a time limit for each hunt; or say it must end when you reach the end of a path or a type of environment. At the end of the hunt, allow some time for them to show their finds and explain why they chose each item especially if they are unusual ones.

Make it even more fun by encouraging competition. Who can find the biggest leaf or the longest feather? Who can find a chewed pine cone?

Do not allow children to:

- Pick wildflowers
- Break branches or plants
- Pick berries, toadstools or mushrooms

Secret Smells

Take – Scarf for use as a blindfold

How well can you recognise the scent of a particular leaf or plant? The scent of elder leaves is very pungent, whereas beech leaves have very little smell. Wild mint, wild blackberry leaves, pine needles and rotting leaves are equally distinctive. The aim is to see if a particular plant can be recognised by smell alone.

Blindfold the child, and then give an aromatic leaf or other aromatic natural material to the child. Encourage the child to smell the object; crumpling it with fingers often releases the aroma at its strongest level.

Similar or different?

Take – An egg box

Give each child an empty egg box. As they walk along, they have to find five items that are similar and one, which is different. As it is found it has to be placed in one of the compartments in the egg box. When all are full, it is time to stop and see what has been found. Either you or another child has to decide which is the item that is different to all the rest; and why the others are all similar.

Older children enjoy making this quite difficult by looking for things that are only slightly different such as having an extra point on a leaf, or a deciduous leaf among evergreen leaves, five pigeon feathers and one from a blackbird.

It is fun activity that encourages children to look closely and observe natural items very closely.

Shrunk

Take: Magnifying glasses and string

What can be seen at insect level? Imagine drinking the 'shrink me' potion in Alice in Wonderland. You could even give the kids a little drink or sweet saying it has shrinking powers. Then down on hands and knees or even onto the stomach to crawl among the grass or bushes. What can be seen? Magnifying glasses can help to see small insects more clearly. Children should remember that the grass is a forest to these tiny insects.

Look out for beetles or ants scurrying along, grubs and centipedes. Caterpillars may be spied munching on leaves. What colour are they? Be careful touching caterpillars – some have hairy bodies that can cause an adverse reaction in some people.

In a grassy meadow, look out for frothy 'cuckoo spit' on grass stems – it may even be possible to see the tiny green froghopper larvae inside. Watch out for silken tents woven among stems to protect baby spiders – do not disturb or break the silken framework. Carefully move around mounds of earth – these may contain ant hills. Watch the ants at work, but beware they can sting – especially red ants.

If you want to encourage the children to go in a specific direction such as the way you propose walking, it can be an idea to ask them to follow a string path that is laid out for them. Lay the string along the ground and walk very slowly on, allowing them plenty of time to explore the path created for them.

If there are several children involved, another slant on the game would be to ask them to find something really, really interesting on their crawl path within a set time of say one minute. When the time is up, they show their find to the rest of the group and explain why they find it so interesting.

Sleeping lions

Find an open spot where children can lie down slightly apart from each other. This reduces the opportunity for giggling! They have to imagine they are lions sleeping in the sun. The game can be played in different ways.

The sleeping lion

Who can be the quietest, unmoving lion?

Choose a child or your- self to act as a tracker. How close up to the 'lions' can you get with-out them seeing you?

Walk on a little, then make a sound. At that point, all the lions have to jump up and start running towards you. How quickly can the 'lions' reach their prey?

Smelly cocktails

Take: Small containers
Find: A stick for each container

This can be done either as you walk along or at a convenient stopping place. The aim is to make a smelly cocktail. Give each child a container and a stick. They have to hunt around for smelly leaves, bits of moss, and anything else that has a scent. This could even include mud, soil, and decaying leaves. Mix them up and see what scent results. Is it pleasant or is it horrible? This could become a bit of a competition eventually – who can make the nicest smelling cocktail? Who can make a really foul smelling one? What does it smell like? Get them to describe the smell – this is a good exercise for encouraging them to think about words and expand their vocabulary.

Keep an eye on what they are including in their mix to make sure they are not touching decaying animals or birds, or including poisonous plants. The biggest danger is in the autumn when mushrooms and toadstools have appeared. Make sure they understand that fungi should not be included – it is not easy to tell which is poisonous and which is not. Many fungi can cause harm simply by touching.

When the game is complete, make sure that all the contents of the containers are emptied away. The containers should be taken home.

Squirrel

Find: A collection of acorns

The robber squirrel

This is a game that is best played in the autumn or winter in location where you start and end the walk in the same place. The aim is to see if you can remember where you buried some nuts. Squirrels bury nuts in autumn – and cannot always remember where they did so. Can you do better?

At the start of your walk, collect up some acorns. These should then be buried under leaves, under a bush or in a hiding place of some kind. Look for any identification pointers as you do so. What trees are near by? Is there a bush in flower? How many steps away from the trunk of a tree? Check too if there are any real squirrels around. They have been known to watch children hiding nuts and then steal them!

Leave the nuts in hiding and go on with your walk. When you return, try and find your buried nuts? How good is your memory? It is not as easy as you might expect. And of course, there is always the risk of a pesky squirrel taking the nuts for its own use!

Stick throwing

Find: A selection of straight sticks
Take: A tape measure might be good idea to resolve arguments!

Collect sticks along the way. Look for sticks that are straight, with no curves or broken pieces. They need to be light yet strong. Aim for a variety of sizes.

When you come to an open area or clearing, have a stick throwing contest. No stick should be thrown in the direction of a person, animal, bird or tree. Remember it can hurt if it hits you.

Before throwing a stick, double check there is no one in the direction the stick is to be thrown. The aim is to throw the stick as far as possible.

The game can be developed in different ways:

Who can throw a stick the longest distance?
To be fair, each player should start on the same spot. Mark the stick in some way – perhaps by tying some grass around it or scratching a mark on the bark. This will enable you to identify your stick. When everyone has thrown their stick, each person goes out to find where their sticks have landed. Once their stick has been identified, they should stand next to it. This will enable you to immediately identify whose stick has travelled the longest distance.

What type of stick is best for throwing?
Experiment by throwing similar size sticks made from different woods. Which type of wood travels the longest? Is there any difference?

Are throwing sticks better if they are straight or slightly bent?

Experiment by throwing different types of sticks and seeing what the results are. Do straight sticks travel better? Do they go further than sticks that have a bend or a twig sticking out?

What size of stick works best?

Do shorter sticks travel further than longer ones?

Whose aim is the best?

Decide on a suitable distance acceptable to everyone. Set up a clearly identifiable target, perhaps a can, bottle or large stone. Who can hit the target first? Who can hit it the most times?

Tracking

Try tracking each other through the undergrowth. Set a marker, say a particular tree which has to be reached before the tracker sees you. This is a good exercise to practise moving very, very quietly and making as little disturbance as possible to the environment.

Give the tracked person a head start, then begin tracking their movements. The moment you see them, call out their name and say where they are. If correct, the child has to start again.

Another variation is for one person to go ahead and place agreed markers such as stones and sticks laid out in the shape of arrows, or drawing arrows in chalk on tree trunks. These markers should be placed at intervals along the path, and at any junction in the path. The children accompanied by an adult should then try and follow the markers. To make it a little more complex, why not add in a few false trails to confuse them?

Initially, the tracked person should only go a short distance before waiting to check the children are on their trail. No one wants to get lost! As children become more adept at this form of tracking, the tracked person can leave longer intervals before stopping. Why not hide in the bushes and catch them unawares or see if they can find you?

When playing these games, make sure that you only use paths, which have public access. Children should always be accompanied by at least one adult, and they should stay in groups rather than wander off alone. Older children should stay in pairs.

Torch game

Take: Torch and blindfold

Ideal for playing in a clearing or open area at dusk or early night. Several players are needed. It encourages children to concentrate on hearing and listening. One child should be blindfolded and given a torch. The rest of the players spread out in a circle. They have to stalk their target and reach the blindfolded child without being heard. If the blindfolded child hears a sound, the child shines the torch in the direction of the sound. If someone is caught in the light, they have to stay still for one minute. The game ends when the blindfolded child is captured.

What's the time Mr wolf?

This is a fun game, which can be played whenever you stop for a few minutes. It can be played with any number of children or adults, and is guaranteed to cause laughter. Playing What's the Time Mr Wolf may take only a few minutes, or it can take much longer, depending on the skill of the children.

One person is named Mr Wolf. All the other players stand in a line some distance away. The object is to reach Mr Wolf without being seen. You have to move very stealthily in a straight line towards Mr Wolf.

Mr Wolf

Mr Wolf stands with his/her back to the rest of the group. The others ask the question "What's the time, Mr Wolf?" While asking the question they can move forwards. Mr Wolf responds by turning round quickly and giving a time. Children have to be very still while he is facing them. If Mr Wolf sees the slightest hint of movement, that person has to go back to the beginning.

Alternatively, Mr Wolf might say "Dinner Time" at which point Mr Wolf runs towards the group and tries to catch 'dinner'. If anyone is caught then they become Mr Wolf.

Word Games

These are all games, which can be played while walking along with any number of players. No equipment is needed, although a little preparation is useful creating lists which can be referred to when necessary. For example, having a list with a few examples of animals, birds or insects beginning with awkward letters like x, y and z does make life easier! The only other exception is the game of Identification, where a book on identifying flowers, trees, shrubs, animal prints is useful.

Add a word

A simple story making game which can involve as many people as you want. Each person adds just one word to the story being created. For example,

Jenny	"Once"
John	"Upon"
Anna	"A"
Mary	"Time"
Jenny	"A"
John	"giraffe"
Anna	"walked"
Mary	"into"
Jenny	"Zebra"
John	"Street"
Anna	"and"
Mary	"watched"
Jenny	"Hippos"

And so on until someone manages to end the story. It can be made as silly, exciting or funny as required.

Alphabet game

The object is to name items from nature in alphabetical order. Much depends on the age of the children – a mixed age group, or if there are young children present it is better to concentrate on choosing

letter a

anything that begins with the appropriate letter whether it be an animal, insect, tree, flower or bird. With older children, you can be more focused choosing just one category such as animals in alphabetical order.

Playing the game is quite simple. The first person to start the game begins with the letter A saying "A is for" and names something from nature such as an antelope. The next person says "B is for ......", this is followed by "C is for....." and so on until the end of the alphabet is reached. It can be quite fun when people start struggling to think of an answer. Being quick-witted helps tremendously. Don't let it drag out too long when people are thinking of answers as this can quickly lead to children's attention waning. Keep the pace of answers as quickly as possible but be prepared to help out with hints such as "something white that flies at night (owl)". This is where having a quick reference list can help.

Alphabet dinner

Create a long list of items that you have to say in alphabetical order or else you are 'out'. The first person starts with the words "Today I had for dinner some" and names a food beginning with A such as Apples.

The next person says "Today I had for dinner some apples and" then adds a food beginning with B like bananas.

Then the third player takes up the list, adding a food beginning with C and so on. Anyone who cannot think of a suitable food or is unable to remember the entire list is out of the game.

Animal, vegetable, mineral

The aim is to guess what another player has chosen. The chooser decides on a specific animal (eg: dog) vegetable (eg: potato) or mineral (eg: stone). Animal is any living creature; vegetable is any type of plant or part of a plant, while mineral is any object that has never been alive.

When walking, a simple version of this is to make it a rule that players can only choose something they can see: this makes children more aware of what they see around them.

Other people present have to try to guess what the object is. They have to ask questions such as: Is it a vegetable? Is it an animal? Does it fly? Is it red? Is it a stone? The chooser can only reply yes or no.

The person who guesses correctly what the object is becomes the next chooser. If no one can guess the correct answer, then the chooser wins and can have another turn.

Avoidance

Choose a player to begin the game. Give that person a word such as cat. Then that player has two minutes to answer questions from everyone else - but has to try to avoid using the word cat. Naturally, everyone else is trying to catch them out by asking questions designed to make them use the word.

If they manage to avoid using the word 'cat' for two minutes, they win that round. It is then someone else's turn to be given a word, and has to answer the questions.

It is a game that requires some concentration, as it is all too easy to forget what you are doing and use the forbidden word!

Beastiary

How much can you say about an animal in a timed span of one minute? Each child chooses an animal such as a rabbit, hedgehog, or badger and then has to talk about it for one minute. But they must not repeat themselves at any point.

Depending on the age and ability of the children, subject matter can be kept as wide or as narrow as you like. You could say that the animals must be woodland animals, or animals of the plains, farm animals or endangered animals. If you are walking on moorlands or along the seashore – the animals chosen must be ones which would live in that environment.

Bird, beast, fish or flower

This is a game best played in a clearing or when you stop for a short rest along the way. The aim of this game is to guess a word from its initial letter. Divide into two teams facing each other some distance apart. The players on one side decide among themselves on a beast, fish, bird or flower. They then go towards the other team and give the first letter of the chosen word, eg: d for dog. If the other team guesses it correctly, the first team turns and runs back to their original position – chased by the second team.

If anyone is caught, then they have to join the second team. It is then the turn of the second team to choose a word. The winning team is the one which gains the largest number of players.

Combination fun

This is a game that older children will enjoy. A sense of humour, and some knowledge of words is essential. The aim is to create sentences which play on words for example:

> Mary "Have you ever seen a kitchen sink?"
> John "Have you seen a tin doing the can can?"
> Jake "Have you herd of cows?"

The jokes can only get worse!

Chinese whispers

Another game for when you are sitting and having a rest. At least four or five people are needed to play this game. The aim of the game is to see how a sentence changes as it passes round the group.

Sit in a circle. Choose a person to begin the game. That person whispers a short sentence into the ear of the person sitting beside them. They then whisper it to the person beside them and so on until the message returns to the person who originally made it up. By this time the message will have inevitably changed.

Earth air water

Quick thinking is needed for this game which is best played in groups of at least four or more. Participants can sit or stand in a circle. One player throws a small light object such as a handkerchief or ball at another person in the circle, shouts "earth", "air" or "water", and starts counting to ten. The other player must name a creature that lives in the chosen environment, eg: possible answers to "air" might be butterfly, wasp, swallow or owl. If no answer has been given by the time the number ten has been reached then the first player has another go, throwing the object to another player. As soon as someone answers correctly, they take the object and ask the question.

To make it slightly more difficult, you could add in the word 'fire'. If the word 'fire' is shouted then the player receiving the object has to remain silent – not always easy in the fun of the game!

Elf taboo

Who can guess the forbidden letter of the alphabet? One player is chosen as the Elf. It is the Elf's task to question the other players. The Elf chooses a letter of the alphabet that is taboo – but does not tell anyone else what it is. The Elf then asks the other players questions that are designed to encourage them to use the forbidden letter. They have to answer using just one word. If the forbidden letter is included, they lose a life. Losing three lives means they are out of the game. If they guess the forbidden letter, then they become Elf for the next turn.

For example:

Elf (having chosen the letter o as taboo) "What day is it?"	
Jenny	"Monday "
Elf	"You lose a life"
Jenny	"Is it a?"
Elf	"No"
Elf	"What time is it"?
John	"ten o'clock"

Elf	"you lose a life"
John	"is it O?"
Elf	"yes"

John now becomes Elf.

Follow on

Two or more people are needed to play this game. It tests spelling skills and quick thinking.

One person starts the game by saying a word such as mouse. The next person has to follow it with a word beginning with the last letter of the previous word - e. So they could choose Eat. The next person has to come up with a word beginning with T and so on.

To make it more difficult, you could choose a theme, like nature, fantasy or art from which words have to be chosen.

Good news, bad news

This game aims to build up stories by alternately using pieces of good and bad news.

So the first player could start with "The good news is that we are going on holiday". The next player says "The bad news is that all the planes are on strike." This is followed by a piece of good news "the good news is that we are going by boat" then bad news "the bad news is that storms are forecast" and so on. The story can go on and on until you run out of ideas!

Grandmother's trunk

This is a popular alphabetical word game involving the creation of an ever-growing list. Begin with the words "My grandmother has an (add a word beginning with the letter A) in her trunk". The next person repeats the sentence and adds something beginning with B.

Sarah   "My grandmother has an apple in her trunk".
Mary   " My Grandmother has an apple and a balloon in her trunk"

Colin   "My Grandmother has an apple, a balloon and a coin in her
        trunk"
Sarah   "My Grandmother has an apple, a balloon, a coin and a dolphin
        in her trunk."

And so on until someone cannot think of an item or gets the list wrong
and is then declared out of the game. The winner is the last person
still listing everything correctly.

How many?

How many words can you find to describe a hedge, field or other
object? This has the added bonus of encouraging language
development.

Be prepared with a selection of words, which can be used to describe
the object. For example, useful words for a hedge include:

> Dense
> Spiky
> Evergreen
> Deciduous
> Damp
> Shady

A church could be described as:

> Grey
> Stony
> Cold
> Towering
> Big
> Norman
> A church with a tower
> A church with a steeple

Who can think of the most words?
This can become quite a competitive
affair as children try to outdo each
other.

church view

Identification

Take: a tree and plant identification book

The aim is to identify as many trees and plants as you can within a specified number of minutes. Start by using the book to help identify say ten plants and trees. Then see how many you can identify correctly using just your memory. This can become quite competitive.

I spy

This is a classic game which appeals to everyone. One person has to decide on an object such as a tree and then say, "I spy something beginning with t". All the other people present have to try and guess what 't' stands for. The person who guesses correctly then chooses an object and asks "I spy something beginning with ?"

This is a game that can last for some time, depending on how many people are playing it. Older children enjoy trying to think up something awkward so as to catch the others out.

Playing the game amid a landscape with plenty of variety will make the game more challenging, as it will offer the widest variety of words. It is a good game for improving spelling.

Younger children can improve their overall vocabulary as they learn new words for things they see along the way.

I went to the market

An alphabetical game requiring you to remember an ever growing list of items.

The first person starts with the words "I went to the market and I bought an aubergine". The next person says, "I went to the market and I brought an aubergine and a bottle." The next person adds something beginning with C and so on until the end of the alphabet is reached.

Anyone who cannot think of an item, or gets the list wrong is out of the game.

Keep talking

How long can you keep talking about a subject without repeating yourself? This is best played with at least three or four players. One person chooses a subject about whom the next person has to talk for 30 seconds without hesitating or repeating themselves. If they do they can be challenged, and if successful, the challenger takes their place. They are then out of the game. At the end of 30 seconds, the next person takes over. The winner is the last person left in the game.

Minister's cat

The minister's cat

A game which helps children to remember the alphabet and also increases their vocabulary. You have to know lots of adjectives or describing words.

To play it, one person says something like "The minister's cat is an amazing cat." The next person has to say the same sentence but replace the word amazing with another adjective beginning with a such as anxious. When all the players have had a go, the next round begins using the letter B eg "The minister's cat is a bashful cat". The game continues until you run out of adjectives or reach the end of the alphabet. Anyone unable to think of a suitable adjective has to drop out of the game.

If you want to make the game more difficult, you can also name the cat as well as giving it a description for example "The minister's cat is an arrogant cat and is named Adam"

Alternatively, players have to include all the adjectives used for example:

Mary   "The minister's cat is an amazing cat"
Barbara   "The minister's cat is an amazing, adorable cat"
Tom   "The minister's cat is an amazing, adorable, awful cat"

Anyone getting the list mixed up or missing adjectives is out of the game.

Missing letters

This is a guessing game which can be played by children of all ages. Just choose the words which are within the child's own capability. Playing it is quite simple. Think of a word, such as dog. Spell it out to the other players missing out the vowel. So you would say d – g? Can you guess the word?

Longer words might need some hints given. For example "What animal is spelt - l - ph - nt?"

The flying albatross

One awkward albatross

This is another alphabet game where the aim is to create the most weird and wonderful (and hard to remember) collection of animals, birds and insects.

The first person begins by saying "one awkward albatross". The next person repeats this and adds a phrase using the letter B such as two blue butterflies. The third player then says "one awkward albatross, two blue butterflies, three crazy cats." Each player in turn adds an item to the list. If they cannot repeat it exactly and add a suitable item, then they are out of the game.

Questions

A challenge game that just requires quick wits to play it. The aim is to answer questions with another question. It can be played by any number of people either in a group or just between two or three people. No repetition or long pauses are allowed. Failure to come up with a question means that the other player is the winner.

Example:

Mary	"What's your name?"
Joe	"Do you mean at home?"
Penny	"Is it different at home?"
Joe	"why?"
Mary	"I don't know do you?"

Riddles

If you are going to play this, you may need a little bit of preparation beforehand. Riddles are not easy to make up on the spot unless you are very quick witted. A riddle basically is a question or statement that is deliberately designed to puzzle you. One person asks the riddle. Others have to guess the answer. For example: "When is a door not a door" The answer is 'ajar'.

Other typical riddles:

> **A box without hinges, key or lid**
> **Yet golden treasure inside is hid.**
> **(Answer an egg)**
>
> **Thirty white horses on a white hill,**
> **First they champ,**
> **Then they stamp,**
> **Then they stand still.**
> **(Answer is teeth).**

Sausages

How long can you keep a straight face without laughing while answering all questions with a silly answer? This is not as easy as you might think. Sausages is a game which tests this skill to the utmost!

First of all, choose a word which everyone agrees is really silly. It could be something like 'sausages' or 'bananas'.

One person is chosen to be questioned. Their task to answer every question with the silly word. The other players have to ask questions for example:

Jenny	"What's your name?"
Mary	"Sausages"
Tom	"What's the date?"
Mary	"Sausages"
Ben	"What do your fingers look like?"
Mary	"Saus......" and collapses in laughter.

Someone else then becomes the person to be questioned.

Simon says

A very traditional game which can cause a lot of laughter. It does need several players. Stand in a ring. One person is the centre and takes on the role of 'Simon' giving instructions using the words "Simon says." Typical instructions might be "Simon says touch your toes", "Simon says jump up and down", "Simon says, hop on one leg". But to catch people out, sometimes instructions are given without using the words 'Simon Says'. If anyone obeys those instructions, they are immediately out. Instructions should be given as quickly as possible so as to increase the chances of a player not listening correctly, or missing the words 'Simon Said'. The last person still following instructions correctly takes on the role of Simon.

Story making

All you need for this game is some imagination as the stories can lead anywhere. It is very easy to play. You just start to tell a story and keep going until someone else interrupts and takes the story over.

For example:

Mary   "Bruin Bear sat on a chair. He was bored and wanted
       something to do".
Jenny "Bruin decided to go for a walk so he put on his coat and
       Wellingtons and went outside".
Mary   "Only to find it was raining so heavily he was soaked before
       he got to the gate. Then he saw Mrs Bear with an umbrella
       and asked if he could share it. They went off down the road
       and found the river had risen over its banks and was flooding
       the road."
Tom   "Then the army came along in big helicopters to lift the bears
       to safety. Unfortunately one of the helicopters broke down"

It is quite fun to include the children's favourite toys in the story
which can take all kinds of different routes from silly to adventurous,
funny to mysterious.

Traveller's alphabet

An alphabet based game in which players have to think of a group of
words starting with a specified letter of the alphabet.

The first player begins using the words "I am going on a journey to
(and chooses a place beginning with the letter A such as Antwerp).
The next person asks, " What will you do there?"

The first player has to answer using three words beginning with A for
example: "I shall attract angry antelopes."

The next player continues the game using the words "I am going on a
journey to (someplace beginning with B).
"What will you do there?"
"I shall begin baking bread"

The questions and answers continue round the group. If someone
cannot answer or think of a suitable location, they are out of the game.
The winner is the last person left in the game.

Tree stories

Look carefully at trees and try and decide what type of person they would be if they could talk. Birches are graceful trees and it is easy to imagine them as light-hearted dancers; Oaks on the other hand are sturdy, majestic trees, kings of the woodland. What descriptions can you create?

Consider too making up stories about trees perhaps using some the tree characters you have been creating. There are lots of legends about trees which can provide ideas.

Typical legends include:

Hazel

Celtic people believed that eating hazelnuts made you wise. They had a story about nine hazel trees which grew around a pool. All their nuts fell into the pool and were eaten by a salmon. As he ate the nuts, he gained all their wisdom. The number of spots on his skin showed just how many nuts had been eaten.

Hawthorn

In some areas of the UK it is regarded as unlucky to take bunches of 'May' (flowering branches of hawthorn) into the house. People used to gather garlands of may blossom to hang around the outside of houses on May Day. Hawthorn trees were also the original May Pole around which people would dance.

Elder

In Denmark, there are legends of a spirit called the Elder-Tree mother, which lives in the branches. If furniture were made from elder wood, the Elder tree mother would follow and haunt the owners. To avoid this, she had to be asked before the wood was cut.

What legends and stories can you make?

What can you see?

A simple game, which can be played as you walk. It tests a child's powers of identification and their ability to notice things. Ask, "How many things can you see?" The aim is to say as many things as possible within the scope of one minute. The person who comes up with the longest list wins.

Yes and no

This is a challenge type game in which you have to answer questions without using the words 'yes' or 'no'. You need to be quick witted and to concentrate so as not to use the forbidden words.

Decide who is going to go first. That person has to answer all questions asked by everyone else in the group without saying 'yes' or 'no' or nodding or shaking their head. Naturally, everyone else is trying to ensure that the other player uses the words as quickly as possible. The winner is the person who manages to survive as long as possible without using the forbidden words and gestures.

Art and Craft

In general, these are activities which require art work to be undertaken on the spot, or to collect up items to complete work at home. Most can be undertaken by children of any age, although some adult help may be required with younger children. Preparation is essential to make sure you have everything needed before setting off on a walk.

Animal footprints

Take: Paper and pencils

Try sketching as many animal footprints as you can find. These can then be combined to create an unusual work of art. Possible ideas could include a painting of footprints along a muddy track? It could be a scene such as a fox's paw prints chasing after a rabbit? Or why not just have footprints wandering all over the page in a random fashion?

Animal footprint casts

Take – Plaster of Paris, strips of cardboard, some water, a jug, spoon, paperclip and wipes for cleaning mucky hands afterwards

Look for a muddy spot in the woodlands. Ideally this should be where several tracks meet, as this is where you are most likely to find lots of animal tracks. Search for an animal footprint that is quite deep and well defined. Take a strip of cardboard and place it in a circle around the footprint, holding it in place with a paperclip. Make up the plaster of Paris using some water. It needs to be a thick, creamy consistency. Pour the mixture into the cardboard framework and leave to set. This will take about 20 minutes. Gently prise the plaster cast out of the ground. Carry it carefully or put it into a small box to take home. It will take at least two to three hours for it to set really hard.

If you want, you can clean it up with a brush removing any dirt, then paint over it using acrylic paints. Add a layer of varnish for a glossy finish. It can make a lovely ornament or paperweight.

Carrying water and plaster of Paris around can be quite heavy so choose your location carefully.

Bark rubbings

Take: Paper, wax crayons or charcoal

This is a very easy activity that children of all ages can do. A young child may need a little help to press down hard enough to gain an imprint.

Find a spot on the trunk of the tree, which is fairly smooth and no obvious lumps or bumps sticking out. Put the paper firmly against the bark and rub hard using charcoal or waxed crayon. This will create an impression of the pattern of the bark.

Every tree has a different pattern on its bark. Some trees can have lots of clear lines, while others can be smoother. Knot holes can give a very interesting effect. By experimenting with bark rubbings from different trees on the same sheet of paper, you can create a very unusual picture to take home.

Alternatively, use several sheets of paper and a variety of coloured crayons to create rubbings in a number of shades. At home, cut these up to make collage materials. Try creating leaf shades, or tree outlines. Cut out a tree and then stick the bark effect leaves on it. Pictures of houses or people could be created the same way, or create your own imaginative design. Such pictures make a lovely reminder of a walk or a nice present to give away.

Once you have experimented with this technique it can be used on other objects in the area such as fence posts, stones. Even leaves can be used for rubbings, but this does require some care and a gentle touch. Rub too hard and you will break the leaf.

Bird's nests

Find: Natural materials such as twigs, grass, and moss

Birds spent hours making nests every spring, carefully weaving twigs, stems and rushes together and lining them with dry grass, mosses and leaves. The weaving creates support for the internal materials, which provide insulation, and protection for the eggs. Nests are very complex structures and it is fun to have a go at replicating what the birds do. It certainly gives you an appreciation of their sheer hard work.

Children love trying to make birds nests. This is an exercise best done in a woodland clearing or near a clump of trees. Point out any nests in the trees around you – these will usually be high up among the branches. Then spend a little time collecting up suitable materials such as twigs, grasses, feathers, stems, rushes, moss, seed heads, bits of sheep's wool or other soft materials such as scraps of animal fur or even dandelion heads.

Kneeling on the ground, the children should take some of the twigs and gently weave them into a circular shape. Weave more twigs and stems into the structure until a cup shaped nest is created. This can then be lined with softer materials such as grass, feathers, moss, and wool. Using fists in a circular twisting motion, gently smooth the centre of the nest to create a sitting place for a bird. Once complete, lift the nest and leave it in a sheltered place. Birds may come and take bits of the nest to make their own.

For a more challenging nest, try making a mud nest. These are made by house martins that take up bits of mud to mould it against the side of a house building. You can try moulding the mud to create a structure against the trunk of a tree. Carefully include an opening on one side.

Christmas decorations

Take: Garden wire and string
Find: Flexible twigs, a selection of small twigs, seeds and berries

Natural materials can create very pretty Christmas decorations. Bend flexible twigs into equal sized triangles. Place two triangles together to create a star shape. Fasten edges together with wire or string. The stars can be tied onto a Christmas tree, or tied together to make a star mobile. For a more colourful effect, spray the stars with gold or silver paint.

Take a piece of garden wire and twist it into a ring. Thread berries and seeds onto it. When the ring is full, twist the two ends together to form a closed ring. Attach a piece of string to the top so that it can be hung.

Christmas lights

Take: A glass jar, garden wire, night lights, glue
Find: Seeds, berries, ivy leaves

Some pre-preparation is needed if this activity is being undertaken during a walk. Each child will need a glass jar. Wind some garden wire around the top of the jar. Secure firmly in place. Attach another piece of wire to act as a looped handle across the top of the jar. Find a spot where there are plenty of seeds, berries and evergreen leaves such as ivy. Allow them to collect up their chosen natural materials. These should be glued onto the sides of the jar. Do not cover the entire surface, unless transparent seeds are being used. The aim is for the candlelight to twinkle out from between the seeds and leaves. Once complete, place a night light in the jar.

The decorated jar can be taken home and placed on a branch outside or on a flat surface indoors.

It can also be very effective if this activity is completed near the end of a walk on a dull or darkening afternoon. Light the candles and let the children carry them for the last part of the walk, helping to illuminate the way. This should only be attempted with older children who can be trusted to carry the lights safely.

Conker chairs

Take: A skewer, matchsticks
Find: Conkers

This is an autumn activity. When walking in woods or forested areas, look for horse chestnut trees. These are easily identified by their very large leaves and spiny seed cases that fall to ground, breaking open to reveal a shiny brown conker inside. Collect the conkers. Using a skewer, make a hole part of the way through at each corner. Push a used matchstick into the holes. Adjust the sticks so that the conker stands upright. This creates a small conker chair that can be added to dolls houses.

Colours

Take: Piece of cardboard covered with double sided sticky tape for each child

This is an activity that offers an opportunity to explore colour in the natural world. There are several variations that can be used for example:

Conker chair

How many fragments of natural colour can you get on the piece of card?

This can be quite competitive among groups of children as they try and get more than their friends. Remember that even soil can be used – soil itself can come in different colours.

Find all the colours of the rainbow

This can be a difficult challenge and younger children may need some help. It is best undertaken during a walk, rather than in just one area. Some colours may be difficult to find. Older children could try putting the colours in the same sequence as colours appear in a rainbow. Can they get it right? It is not as easy as you might think! The argument generally results over white – the colour into which others fade.

Make a mosaic out of natural colour

Take natural materials such as leaves, grasses, and common wild flowers like daisies or ragged robin. Break them into even sized pieces and then use them to make a mosaic picture.

How many shades of a specific colour can be found during a walk?

Choose a colour such as brown or green and set out to find as many shades as possible during the walk.

Colour comparisons

Aim for at least two very differing natural environments such as an open meadow and dense woodland. Find as many shades of a colour such as green in one area, and then do the same in the second area.

What differences can be seen? Which area has the most lighter greens or the darkest ones? Why do these differences occur?

Corn dollies

Take: Some raffia or string, scissors
Find: Left over bits of straw

This is very much a summer activity. Look for cornfields that have recently been harvested. At the edges of the cornfield, you will often find left over ears of wheat and pieces of straw. These can be gathered up and made into a corn dolly. This is a task that has a long history. For centuries, people have taken the last of the straw and plaited it into all kinds of shapes such as a doll, knots, fans or lanterns. These were then hung in the kitchen until the next harvest. It was believed that the dollies embodied the crop's spirit and by keeping them safely would ensure a good harvest the following year.

Making a simple corn dolly is easy. Take a handful of corn stems and tie them together. Use the scissors to trim the ends. Divide the bunch of corn into two, tying a piece of string around the middle. This forms the body of the dolly. The lower half should then be divided into two so as to form legs, bending a little at the bottom to create feet. Tie with raffia or string. Then take a thinner bunch of stalks and tie at both ends. Attach this bunch at right angles to the body so to create arms. Weave in grasses or seeds to provide decorations.

Corn dolly

Older children could try plaiting several stalks together to create arms and legs. This does require a little more patience and time. The tighter the plait, the better the overall effect.

Crowns

Take: A piece of thin cardboard– it should be long enough to go around a child's head. Double sided sticky tape
Find: Leaves, berries and other natural materials

Form the cardboard into a circle and staple the two edges together. Attach strips of double sided sticky tape along the crown. Collect lots of natural materials such as pine needles, leaves, berries and seeds. Arrange the chosen items on the sticky tape and press into place.

This activity is particularly good during the autumn when using brightly coloured leaves creates a stunning effect.

Daisy chains

Find: some daisies

Making daisy chains particularly fascinates little girls and with a little bit of practice longer and longer chains can be made, creating crowns, necklaces and bracelets galore. The same technique can be used with buttercups.

Daisies and buttercups are the only wildflowers that can be picked anywhere you go. They are widely available from spring right through to late autumn. The flowers are easy to identify – daisies have golden centres surrounded by a ring of white petals; while buttercups are golden yellow in colour with slightly cupped, shiny petals. They can be found in lawns, fields, woodlands and any patch of waste land.

Find a patch of grass with lots of daisies and/or buttercups. Pick flowers with long stalks. You only need about five flowers to begin a daisy chain. Sit down and carefully make a slit in the stem of each of the daisies. This can be done with a thumbnail. The slit needs to be just big enough to allow another stem to be inserted through it. To make a chain, take one stem and push another stem through the hole you have made thus making a chain of two daisies.

Repeat this process, adding another daisy to the end of the chain by pushing it through the stem of the previous one. When you have a chain big enough to encircle a wrist or neck, join them together to make a circle. A bit of patience is needed at the beginning.

Drawing

Take: Paper and pencils

Many children like drawing and colouring. Take a small drawing book and pencils with you for use when you stop for a break.

Encourage drawing from nature. What shapes can they see? A tree can become an oblong, topped by a square or a semicircle. A bush might be a square, or possess a heart shaped leaf. Try drawing the shapes onto paper. Look closely at shapes in the bark of trees – what sort of faces do they suggest? Old, young, shapely, angry or happy? Can they draw the faces?

Dream catchers

Take: Wool or string for tying
Find: A twig that can be bent into a hoop, a selection of natural materials

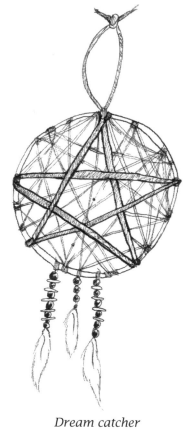

In North America, Native Americans believe that placing a web of natural fibres near a bedside will trap bad dreams, allowing only good ones to reach the sleeper. The dream catcher is always pretty with lots of feathers and seeds, making it an attractive decoration. They are easy to make and are a good activity during a countryside walk or a walk in a park.

To make a dream catcher find a supple twig that can be easily bent into a circle or oval. It can be small or large depending on preference. Tie the ends firmly together. Then tie a long piece of wool or string across the centre of the dream catcher. Pass the wool or string round the outside of the frame, and bring it back to the other side. Repeat

Dream catcher

this exercise two or three times depending on the size of the hoop. This will create a web inside the twig framework.

At the top of the hoop, attach a loop of wool or string. This will be used to hang up the dream catcher. Two or three slightly longer straight threads of wool can be added to dangle loosely below the framework of the dream catcher.

Along the walk, find natural items to attach to the dream catcher. It could be feathers, pretty leaves, grasses, nuts or seeds. Weave these through the web or tie onto the longer straight threads. Grasses could even be woven around the outside of the ring.

Environmental art

Take: A camera to take pictures of the resultant art work
Find: A selection of natural materials

This is a fun activity which can be undertaken anywhere. The materials will vary according to the locality. Materials available on the beach will be very different to those available in a forest or by a river. All it needs is some natural objects and imagination.

Andy Galsworthy is the most well known artist working in the field of environmental art. He has created numerous art works including ice sculptures and leaf designs. The whole aim of environmental art is to create pictures and images which are about the environment and use only natural materials. Once made, the art works are left in place and allowed to degrade and return to nature. The works can be small or large.

All kinds of art work can be created in this way. You can try doing pictures on the ground using leaves, twigs and stones to create images. Alternatively try creating a sculpture using larger branches, fallen logs, leaves and other natural materials. Build up small structures to resemble a tree, or a green man or a home for elves.

Or you can use your imagination to create images which resemble walkers or have a message about the countryside – such as climate change, people damaging the landscape. Consider creating images of the elements – wind, rain, hail, and sunshine. The options are extremely wide.

It is an activity which can become very engrossing, making participants think about the environment and what they are creating. Once completed, take a photo as your permanent memento. Then leave the design for other people to see, and let it slowly return to the environment.

Feather art

Find: Lots of feathers

This is an activity that has to be completed at home unless you are prepared to bring paints and paper with you.

Collect up as many feathers as you can find. Once you start looking, you will many different types – small downy feathers, long pointed ones, thin ones, and fat ones. When you return home, try painting with feathers. Dip the feathers in the paint and brush across the paper. Try doing small strokes with the tips of feathers, or using them like quills. If treating a feather as a quill, it is advisable to sharpen the end using a knife. Experiment with techniques and see what type of picture results.

Feather

Forest mobiles

Take: Collecting bag, large eyed needle, varying lengths of string, a skewer
Find: Seeds, leaves, feathers, a stick at least 30 cms or 12 inches long

This is an activity that can be undertaken during a rest break on a walk, or later when you return home having collected seeds, leaves and feathers along the way.

While walking, look for pretty feathers, leaves, pine cones, berries, and acorns. Only choose seeds and berries that are in plentiful supply. Using the skewer pierce holes through the centre of each item. This may need to be undertaken by an adult. Tie a knot at one end of a piece of string and thread the string through a selection of items. Threading the string using a needle may be easier if the holes are narrow. Try to vary colours and content; mixing leaves with seeds, berries and feathers. There should be a mixture of heavy and light items on each piece of string.

Tie the strings at intervals along the stick. For a more complex design you can attach smaller pieces of string to smaller sticks, then attach these to the main stick.

Attach one long piece of string to both ends of the stick so as to make a handle. This can be hung from a tree along the path so that everyone passing can enjoy it, or take it home and hang it in the garden. Birds will love perching on the mobile to reach the seeds and berries.

Safety Note – check berries and seeds first to make sure nothing poisonous is being included. Make sure that children wipe their hands afterwards.

Flower making

Take: Strips of brightly coloured paper or strips of plastic bag, piece of wire or bendy wood

This can be done anywhere along a walk, but is particularly good in a clearing or meadow.

Start with strips of green paper. These will act as the stem of the flower. Fold up the paper strip like a concertina. Push the wire or bendy wood through the folded paper and push it down almost to the end of the wire. Add more folded pieces of paper, pushing them down to rest on top of the previous ones. Slowly build up a green 'stem'. Then add folded strips of other coloured paper to build up the flower head. Leave about half an inch at the top of the wire. Pull the wire down to form a circle, touching the top of the stem. Twist the wire round the stem. This creates the flower.

The amount of time it takes to make a flower will depend entirely on how tightly you pack the folded paper strips onto the wire.

Why not make a bunch of 'flowers' to take home?

Flower and leaf pressing

Take: Collecting bag
Find: Flowers and leaves

Collect examples of flowers and leaves whilst on the walk. Choose only flowers that are widely available so as to avoid rare plants. At home, press these dry. This can be done using a flower press or by putting the flowers between layers of blotting paper and held down by several large, heavy books. Leave until the flowers and leaves are dry. Use the dried flowers to create collages, birthday cards or bookmarks. Stick onto paper or card, cover with varnish or clear sticky backed paper.

Green man

Take: Camera
Find: Natural materials such as twigs, leaves, grass

This is a variant on Environmental Art. The Green Man is a legendary figure, which guards the countryside, particularly woodlands. They can be found in many legends and stories. Traditionally the Green Man was portrayed as a face covered with leaves and twigs. Often it was a creature hiding in trees, or bushes. Try recreating

The Green Man

a Green Man face using only natural materials. Collect up leaves, twigs, moss, stones and other natural materials. Place these on the ground and form a face. It might have a long mossy beard, or mossy hair. Leaves could be growing out of the cheeks. Blue flowers could form the eyes, and a stone for the nose. It can be made more three dimensional if you clump up the leaves and grass, moulding them to form facial ridges.

When complete take a photograph and then leave the Green Man for others to see. It will slowly decay and return back into the landscape.

Ice castles

Take: Warm gloves
Find: Pieces of ice

Create an ice castle using pieces of ice. Carefully place pieces of ice on top of each other to build the shape of a small castle. Think of Narnia and the White Witch's castle – perhaps tiny pieces of ice could be turned into icy fauns and animals.

Ice creatures

Take: Warm gloves
Find: Pieces of ice, natural materials such as stones or moss

Use pieces of ice to form the outline of an ice creature. Add stones or moss to give hair, eyes, nose, and mouth. Small twigs could be used for fingers. The scope for this activity is wide ranging as sculptural possibilities could include ice people, animals, imaginary creatures, ice dragons as well as scenery such as trees and mountains. Once in place, take a picture and leave the creature for others to see and enjoy.

Journey sticks

Take: Card or stick, wool, strips of fabric
Find: Natural objects like berries, leaves, small twigs

The aim is to tell the story of your walk, finding materials and colours that reflect the various locations and environments along your path.

There are various ways this can be done.

The simplest is to take with you a piece of card to which a strip of double sided adhesive tape has been added. At intervals along the walk collect a leaf, a petal, tiny twig or other item that sums up that part of the journey. Stick this onto your card. By the end of the journey your card will be full.

Alternatively take with you a small bag containing strips of wool or fabric. At the beginning of the walk choose a medium sized stick. It should not have branches sticking out from it, but be fairly smooth and straight. It should be large enough for the child to handle easily. At intervals along your walk, pick up a natural object such as a leaf which sums up that spot and tie it onto your stick using a piece of wool or fabric.

Another variation on the journey stick concept would be to tie wool or fabric of various colours to the stick. The colours represent the environments through which you pass. So for example, you pass a river or stream tie on something blue. Passing through a patch of buttercups, tie on some bright yellow material. A thickly wooded area with little natural light might be identified by the use of some deep brown or black wool.

This concept can be adapted to suit any environment whether it is woodland, seashore or even walking through a town.

This is an activity that encourages children to think about their walk, and what colours and items sum up different environments. The hardest part is encouraging them to space out their collecting otherwise they will fill up their journey stick before the walk is over!

Leaf fun

Take: Paint and paper
Find: Lots of leaves

Leaf prints make a fantastic picture and are easy to do. Leaves are best obtained on a dry, sunny day in autumn when the leaves have been falling thickly from the trees. Collect up a selection of different types of leaves. Avoid getting any that are too dry as these will crumble up and not make very good leaf prints. Aim for ones that have recently fallen.

On returning home, paint over the front of each leaf with paint. Turn it over and press the painted side onto a sheet of plain paper. Gently remove the leaf and see the imprint left behind. Experiment with different shaped leaves to create pictures. You could even try creating your own leaf person – print a rounded leaf for a face, a longer leaf for the body, thin leaves for the arms and legs. Draw in features such as hair, ears, eyes, nose and mouth or glue on leaves and grass.

Use leaves as a stencil. Carefully draw round the outside of the leaves with a pencil. When the leaf is removed, it leaves an outline of the leaf. This can be coloured in, decorated with seeds or fabric, turned into a face or any other thing the imagination can devise.

Magic carpets

Find: Four long sticks, lots of autumn leaves, berries and seeds

The aim is to create a magic carpet of colour that can take you to an imaginary world.

Lay the sticks in place to make a rectangle. Fill the rectangle with leaves, seeds and berries. The design can be random or highly stylised. Use patterns, or create a picture such as a ship, tree or bird. Once complete, take a photo of it so that you have a permanent record of what has been done. Sit on the carpet and make up stories as to where it takes you – a land of mischievous pixies, battles on the high seas, a land where dragons fly free, pirate adventures or mysteries. Leave the carpet design for other

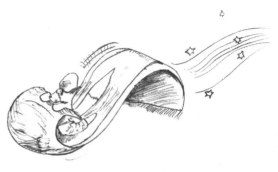

Flying with magic

people to see and admire. It will eventually decay and return to the natural environment.

Masks

Take: Cardboard mask outlines, glue sticks or double sided sticky tape, string or thin elastic to use as ties
Find: Natural materials

Cardboard mask outlines need to be created in advance. These could be very simple versions to go round the eyes, or face masks in the shape of animals. A Green Man face mask can also look very effective.

During the first part of the walk, children can collect up items such as grass, leaves, and bits of wool. Find a convenient spot to sit down for a while during which children can stick their found materials on the mask outline. Masks could be colour themed, designed to reflect the season or the animal, or be very imaginative. Think of fairies, elves, highwaymen. The options are endless.

When the mask is fully decorated, make two small holes at either side. Thread elastic or string through them to use as tie to keep the mask in place.

Mud art

Take: Camera, cardboard, wipes for cleaning hands afterwards!

Mud Sculptures
Find a muddy area. Use sticks and hands to mould the mud into shapes and small sculptures. The mud can be rolled into balls, or shaped into figures. Decorate with natural materials such as leaves, moss, twigs, and grass. Leave these to dry and eventually decompose back into the environment.

Mud Pies
Shape mud into a pie shape. This looks particularly effective if there are different shades of mud available, or use alternate layers of mud/leaves/twigs. You could even add a twig candle or two on top of the pie.

Mud pictures

Using fingers scoop up some mud and then use it to 'paint' onto cardboard. Aim to create a simple design such as geometric shapes, a tree or a pattern. As the mud dries some of it will fall away. What will be left on the cardboard is a faded impression of the picture you have drawn.

Cardboard works better than paper for this activity as it is a firmer surface. Paper can be used, but more care needs to be taken not to make it too wet and soggy.

Mud and stick drawing

Use a stick to draw pictures in the mud. This should preferably be a long enough stick that the child can draw without kneeling in the mud! Simple outlines and patterns work best, rather than aiming for too detailed a picture. Add some leaves and other natural items to create a natural collage.

Music making

Take: String for tying, small box or bag
Find: Small branches, twigs, stones and other natural items

This activity is best started in a clearing, but can be continued as you walk on. Be inspired by the sound of the countryside and try to copy them. Create simple musical instruments such as drums, harps, guitars from pieces of wood, stones gathered during the walk. A collection of stones or crisp autumn leaves put into a small box makes a wonderful shaker, while branches can be strung together and plucked like a guitar or harp. Use a stick to tap out rhythms on a tree trunk or hollow log. Find out how many different sounds can be made. Tapping on a living tree will make a different sound to a dead one or a hollow log. Rustling piles of autumn leaves makes a very pleasant sound but how does it differ to the sound made by piles of pine cones or pine needles?

Netting cloaks

Take: Short lengths of garden netting big enough to wrap around a child as a cloak. String may be needed for tying

Find: Natural materials like leaves, bracken, grass

Explore the world of camouflage by making a netting cloak. This enables children to discover what works best when they are trying to blend into the environment.

Collect lots of natural materials such as leaves, small twigs, bracken, grass. Weave these through the netting or tie them to it with string. This can be a bit fiddly, which means younger children will need adult help.

When complete, see if it works. Sit in a corner or near a bush and drape the cloak around you. If you blend in with the environment, then you have succeeded in making good camouflage.

Paint making

Take: Containers, water, strainer, paper and paintbrushes
Find: Stick, stone or something similar to use as a pestle and mortar when grinding the natural materials

The natural world has always been a source of inspiration for dye pigments. Everyone has heard how prehistoric people used berries and similar materials to create cave paintings. Until quite recently, natural materials were the only ways in which clothes could be dyed in various colours.

Children can have a lot of fun making their own pigments out of natural materials. It offers lots of scope for experimentation but can get very, very messy. Some materials such as blackberries and elderberries can stain clothing so make sure that only old clothing is worn during this activity.

Materials can be collected along the way and taken home to turn into paints. Alternatively, it can be done in a clearing or meadow providing you are willing to carry the various containers.

Encourage the children to collect up different materials to find out what dyes can be created.

Good materials for experimentation include:

Blackberries	purple/red colour
Wild raspberries	reddish colour
Elderberries	purple/blue colour
Grass	green
Leaves	green shades
Damson	dark red
Silver birch bark*	purple
Young shoots of bracken	yellow/green shades
Ivy leaves	green
Larch needles	brown
Walnut shells and nuts	dark brown
Young bramble shoots	black
Young shoots of heather	olive yellow
Pine cones	reddish yellow

 * this can be quite hard to do

To create natural dyes:

Place one material at a time inside a container. Grind the material using a stick or stone to release the colour pigments. Add a little water if necessary.

Does the material produce the expected colour? Some materials may produce a very deep colour, others will be much subtler and harder to extract.

If you want a smooth paint, pass the liquid through a strainer. This will remove any bulky material.

Natural pigments can be used to create pictures on paper. Alternatively you could try decorating large leaves, stones or pieces of bark.

Older children might like to try dying pieces of cloth using natural pigments. For this purpose, the pigments will need a fixative in order to stay true to their colour. Alum can be purchased from chemists or alternatively use some tea. Add this to the pigment and mix well.

Safety note

When choosing natural materials for pigments, do not use any poisonous berries or plants. If in doubt, do not use.

Make sure that children wash their hands thoroughly after this activity. They should not taste the dyes or put their hands into their mouths while making dyes.

Pine cones

Take: A bag to carry pine cones

Search for pine cones as you walk. Look for different shapes and sizes. At home, these can be painted gold and silver to be used as Christmas decorations.

Alternatively, use modelling clay to make heads, arms and legs and turn them into pine people or pine animals.

Attach some string to a pine cone. Cover the cone with a thick layer of vegetable fat and seeds. In the winter time, hang the cone in a tree. Birds love it as it provides much needed food during cold months.

Pixie homes

Find: Leaves, twigs, moss and other natural materials

This is best undertaken in woodlands or along hedgerows. Use the base of tree trunks, among the gaps where roots go deep into the earth. Other good spots include tree stumps, broken logs, a hole in the ground. Let each child choose the spot they prefer. Then, using whatever materials are to hand such as moss, twigs and leaves, construct a little pixie house and/or garden. Perhaps the front door backs onto a tree stump and is outlined by twigs, with a little path of leaves leading up to it. Small pine cones could make trees in the garden, while berries add a touch a colour.

This activity is particularly fun to do in places where you walk regularly. Children will love coming back to see their houses and see what has happened to them. It can create the start of a story about the pixies, or even be developed into a miniature village on future visits. Going to see the pixie houses can become a reason for going for a walk.

Seed mandala

Take: Piece of card and string, lard or vegetable fat
Find: Small seeds and berries

Collect lots of small seeds and berries. Cover the card thickly in lard or vegetable fat. Arrange the seeds and berries on it so that they are held firmly in place. Pierce a hole in the top of the card and thread some string through it. Hang it from a tree so that the birds can come and eat the seeds and fat during the winter.

Snow sculpting

Take: Camera

A form of environmental art, this involves using snow to form animals or scenes. These can be left flat on the ground, or made three-dimensional by gathering snow into large clumps. With a little bit of imagination, snow can be used to create almost anything. A hedgehog for example can be made out of carefully shaped snow with lots of short sticks poking out of its back. Once completed, take a photo for a permanent reminder then leave the snow sculpture for other people to enjoy as they pass by.

Spiders webs

Take: A piece of black card, glue, spray paint

Cards and pictures using spider's webs can be extremely effective. Delicate, yet strong and very intricate; spiders webs possess a very special beauty. Webs are most noticeable on frosty autumn or winter days when they link plants and shrubs. Look for webs that do not have any spiders or flies on them. Cover the piece of black card with a thin layer of glue. Put the card gently underneath the web. Carefully press the card up against the web. Once the web is touching the glue, gently

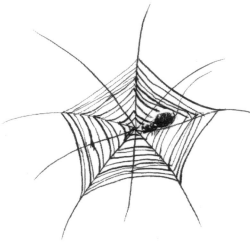

Spiders web

move the card upwards, pulling the web away from the plant. If done carefully, the web will remain stuck to the card, just as it appeared on the plant.

For added decoration, you can try spray painting the area around the web, and a different colour for the web itself. Alternatively someone with a lot of patience and a sure hand, could try using a fine paintbrush to paint the individual lines of the web.

Stained glass windows

Take: Card and sticky backed plastic

Some preparation is needed beforehand for this activity. Cut the centre out of a piece of card so that the cardboard acts as a frame. This could be any shape you like, although it looks most effective when cut into an arch shape. Cover the centre of the card with sticky backed plastic.

Attach petals, pieces of grass and leaves to the sticky backed plastic to make a picture. Try and choose fragments of natural materials that are thin and allow some light to pass through. Grass can make a useful framework in the same way that lead is used in stained glass windows.

Streamers

Take: Some long sticks, long pieces of lightweight fabric or ribbon, glue

This is a fun activity for windy days in open areas such as moorlands, parks, fields and commons. The streamers are simple to make. Tie or glue lengths of fabric to a long stick. Held out in the wind, the fabric

Blowing in the wind

will stream out. Children love walking or running along letting the streamers fly out behind them.

Tree people

Find: Natural materials

Imagination and a close eye for detail will make this activity fun. As you walk through woods or past trees, look out for unusual details that suggest a face or person captured in the tree. Is there something that resembles an eye, a mouth, an arm, claws or horns? When you find something, use natural materials such as grass, moss or twigs to enhance it and bring out other facial features. Having created your tree person, leave it for others to enjoy.

Twig sculptures

Find: Twigs, grasses and pieces of ivy or honeysuckle

Almost anything can be created using twigs including animals, birds, butterflies, fairy tale homes, seats, tables, Green Men and

Green Women, pixies, elves and gnomes. All it needs is a bit of imagination.

Collect up lots of dead twigs and small branches as well as long grasses and pieces of ivy. Combine these together to form the main supports of the sculpture. Use grasses and lengths of honeysuckle or ivy to bind twigs together or to weave in and out of the branches.

Very simple structures can be made easily within a few minutes. Adding some weaving and binding pieces together takes more time, and can require patience to get it right. This is perhaps something that is better undertaken by older children. Younger children would need adult help to complete any weaving of grasses into the sculpture.

Having completed the sculpture leave in place for other people to enjoy.

Woodland collages

Find: Natural materials

Collect natural objects such as dead leaves, small twigs, and bits of moss. Take these natural objects home and use to make a collage. Glue the items onto a piece of card to make a picture. It could be a general picture, a theme, or even the story of the walk.

What to look for

Using eyes and ears as you walk encourages greater observational skills and more awareness of the environment around you.

Talk to your children about what is around them. Identify animals, trees and birds. Some simple guidebooks can help. Look out for animals on your travels. In the wild, the most common are rabbits, foxes, deer, mice, rats and birds.

Why not collect up objects found along the walk and create a nature table at home? This could be regularly changed according to the seasons. Children love collecting items and this can encourage them to go further as they hunt for something new or special. Perhaps they could try and find something new each time they go out? It also helps develop their skills in presentation and display as they need to show off their collection properly, labelling and identifying specimens. Such a nature table could include leaves, disused nests, bones, feathers, animal footprint casts and drawings, pellets, seeds.

Alternatively, flat objects like feathers could be stored inside clear plastic sleeves in folders. Smaller seeds and grasses can be glued onto card. Flowers and leaves can be pressed and dried, then displayed on card.

Animal tracks

Look for animal tracks in muddy areas such as the edges of ponds, pools and along muddy tracks. Areas where tracks cross will usually show signs of animal activity. Animal tracks are also easy to follow when there has been an overnight fall of snow as they stand out very clearly. The fresher the tracks the more they will stand out. Many animals follow the same paths on a regular basis, travelling between their dens and feeding areas.

How many can you identify? Most animal and nature books will show designs of numerous animal paw and hoof prints. The most common are rabbit, fox, deer, horses and birds.

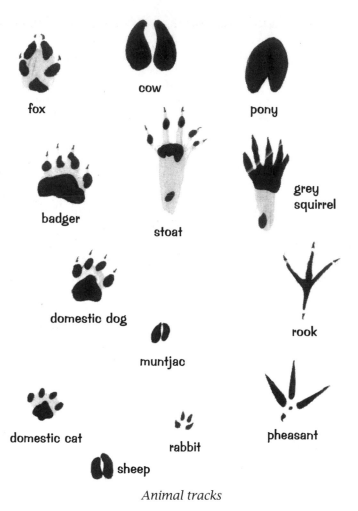

Animal tracks

Try to see how far you can track a particular animal. If the track is really good, you may find yourself walking some distance!

Birds

Take a pair of binoculars and see how many birds can be spotted. The binoculars will enable children to get a much closer view of a bird than is usually possible. They will enjoy using the binoculars to get a view of treetops and clouds as well as birds. If there are any bird hides on the way, slip inside and watch through the slits. Again binoculars will help give a closer view. Using binoculars can encourage children to develop an interest in bird watching. But remember to remind children that they must be very quiet and not frighten the birds away.

Wetlands and estuaries are good places to look for a wide range of over wintering birds, while open fields often attract large numbers of wild geese.

Buildings

Watch out for disused buildings and try to work out what they were used for. While it may be familiar buildings such as sheds, barns, windmills or houses, remember that there may also be the unfamiliar such as Second World War pill boxes to be found across the landscape. As you walk, look for the outlines of buildings on the skyline. How many can you recognise?

This helps children identify where they are, helping them develop a sense of location and find their own way around places.

Windmill

Feathers

Everywhere birds go, they leave some feathers behind. Birds moult gradually, changing feathers one at a time. Children enjoy making a collection of feathers. Encourage them to look at the different colours and sizes. How many different types can they find? What differences can they see for example soft downy feathers from a bird's body and the tough flight feathers from wings.

Fossils

Many children will enjoy searching for fossils. The most obvious fossils are usually found on seashores where the remains of prehistoric insects, sea creatures and animals may be found etched in stone. Fossils can be found inland too – examine stones carefully for the markings of insects or shells. In areas of flint, you might even find arrowheads or sharp stones used by prehistoric man. Keen eyes are needed. Guidebooks are useful in helping to work out whether a fossil has been found. Many local museums are willing to look at such finds when presented by children and give their opinions as to identity and age.

Ammonite

Hollow trees

Look for hollow trees in woodlands. Children enjoy being able to actually get inside a tree. It offers lots of potential for games and creating stories. Encourage them to look closely at the inside of the tree – cracks and crannies can act as homes for numerous insects.

Scarecrow trails

These are becoming increasingly popular particularly during the summer and early autumn. Enterprising villages and rural areas make up numerous scarecrows on all kinds of themes and put these up along trails that can take an hour or more to

Scarecrow

complete. Children love trying to find all the scarecrows and guess what they are supposed to represent. It keeps their attention and they forget how far they are walking!

Sculpture trails

Many woodlands and common land in public ownership now incorporate pieces of sculpture such as animals, totem poles, and Green Men all made out of natural materials. Typical of these woodlands are the Forest of Dean which has a long established sculpture trail while Thetford Forest, Suffolk has a range of sculpted animals that can be found. At Dunston Common near Norwich there is a trail, which can be followed giving access to various giant musical instruments such as a xylophone that can be played with a mallet.

Children gladly go on such trails that can be several miles in length as they love to see how many things they can find. The unusual sights add extra interest to the walk.

Signs of animals

Keen eyes are required to see signs of animals. Look for nibbled and half eaten pine cones, which lack all scales – signs that a squirrel has been around. In the autumn look under trees for chewed shells of nuts. This can provide clues as to the identify of the animal who has been eating them – for example, a squirrel will break nuts in half, while a mouse or vole will gnaw a hole in them.

Groups of round, hard droppings usually in an open area – this is likely to indicate that there are rabbits in the area

Look for signs of animal burrows for example:

Rabbits create underground warrens with lots of entrances. These are often in the sides of banks or hills but can be found underground in woods and fields. There may be shallow scrapes nearby with evidence of droppings near the holes.

Fox's dens are often created out of old rabbit or badger sets. They tend to be much deeper into the ground and may be found deep in forests or woodland. There may be tracks, droppings or bits of reddish wool on the ground or nearby branches. A strong smell around the hole usually indicates the presence of a fox.

Badgers setts are found in woodland and may be quite deep. Other openings will be nearby. Look for the remains of bedding outside the main entrance. Badgers clean out their sets regularly. The sets are wider than those of a rabbit, and more of a semi circle. Droppings are left in shallow holes outside the set.

Molehills – these can be found anywhere but are most noticeable in fields and open areas. The piles of waste earth thrown up at regular intervals show the presence of moles. Molehills are ideal for investigating as the moles throw up items from underground. There can be pottery, bones, and roots. Fresh molehills are also useful as you can see tracks of passing animals such as foxes or rabbits.

Mole hill

Encourage the children to try and work out who lives in the various holes and dens. Look for tracks, scraps of wool and droppings to provide clues.

Bird pellets – these are formed from the bits of food that the bird cannot digest. The pellets are coughed up out of its beak. They are found mainly around nesting or feeding areas. The pellets vary in size according to the size of the bird, and what it has been eating. An owl pellet may be around 2-3 cm wide and 4-6 cms long, rook 2-3 cms long, whereas a pellet from a kestrel may be 3-5.5cm long and 1.5-2cm wide. Owl pellets will contain bones and feathers, a kestrel's pellet fur but no bones, while that of a rook will only have grit and plant remains.

Seasons

All seasons – look for scraps of wool on gateposts, fences and wire. This can indicate the presence of foxes, badgers, rabbits, and sheep. In fields where sheep have been grazing, there may be pieces of wool on the ground. Explore the feel of the wool – is it oily, rough, soft, matted?

Lots of feathers on the ground – this may indicate that birds were fighting, or a predator was having a meal. There may also be other remains to be seen such as pieces of bone.

Look for different types of feathers. No two feathers are the same. Some may be soft downy feathers, others are long and strong. Colours range from all shades of brown and black to white, blue, yellow, green and red. How many different types can be found?

Spring – springtime is the season of new growth. Children can have great fun looking for the first signs of spring. Who can be the first to spot new leaves appearing on trees or hedges? Look for buds about to break into leaf. Look too for flower buds since some trees and bushes come out in flower before the leaves such as blackthorn and flowering cherry.

Summer – in long grass look for animal runs – little tunnel shaped runs in the grass, which are made by mice and voles. Watch out for the nests of harvest mice. These are made of grass leaves woven around long grass stems, high off the ground.

Autumn – what can you see in autumn? The approach of autumn is heralded by the sight of leaves beginning to change colour, from green to shades of yellow, red, brown and orange.

Animals and birds will be particularly busy at this time as they feast and gather up stores to see them through the winter. Squirrels will be searching for nuts and berries, while hedgehogs will be keen to eat as much as possible ready for hibernation.

Birds too will be eating ravenously, often as a way of building up body fat to see them through long migration flights. Flocks of birds may be seen gathered on telegraph wires, or on the branches of trees as they get ready to fly away. Other birds will be arriving from more northerly areas, ready to settle into their winter homes.

Look for pine cones nibbled by squirrels or mice. If squirrels have been feeding on cones, they will leave them scattered underneath the tree. Woodpeckers also like pine cones but tend to split the seed scales as they eat.

Toadstools and mushrooms may show evidence of squirrels and mice. Look – but do not touch – to see if teeth marks can be seen.

Look out for edible berries. Blackberries are delicious. Choose bushes set away from the road. Collect berries to take home to make pies, crumbles and smoothies as well as eating berries straight from the bush. Have some wipes at hand as they can get very messy! Children will also enjoy searching for sweet chestnuts for roasting, while crab apples and sloes can be turned into jellies.

Brambles full of blackberries may reveal evidence of a fox nearby. Foxes have been known to sit in bramble patches, eating the berries. Look for flattened areas and possibly bits of reddish fur. Sometimes a fox can even be seen moving away from a bramble patch. They have also been known to gorge themselves on crab apples.

Fallen fruit can attract wasps. At this time of the year, they tend to be easily angered and stings are common and painful.

Horse Chestnut trees are always a delight for children. The shiny conkers provide hours of fun.

Conkers

Winter – this is a good time to identify evergreen trees as these stand out clearly in the winter weather. Look for other plants such as mosses, which retain their colour in wintertime.

Going out to hunt for animal tracks immediately after a night time snowfall can result in long walks, as children love tracking the varied animals through the snow. Tracks stand out clearly against the snow – paw and hoof marks as well as evidence of tails dragging along.

Squirrel dreys stand out clearly against the winter sky. Look for these high in trees, usually around a fork in the tree. Built of twigs and lined with feathers, moss, grass and fur the drey looks like a large round enclosed birds nest.

Look at trees to see if animals have been eating the bark. Fallow deer pull off strips of bark. Squirrels and rabbits also attack the bark, but tend to leave smaller teeth marks.

Watch out for spiders webs on frosty or icy days. These are beautifully outlined against the vegetation making their intricate lines and patterns clearly visible.

Ladybirds, lacewings and spiders often shelter inside hollow stems or cracks in the bark of trees. If spotted, they should not be disturbed.

Squirrels can often be seen chasing up and down trees, scurrying across the ground hunting for their winter nut supply.

Things to do

This chapter aims to provide lots of ideas for general activities that can be undertaken while out and about on a walk. Many of the activities are based on nature and discovering more about the surroundings through which you are going.

Be a detective

Take: String, magnifying glass, pen and paper

This is a way of getting children to investigate very closely a small area of land. It can be used in any environment - woodland, parkland, and fields. Try setting a time limit and doing comparisons with other areas further on in the walk.

Take a piece of string about 2m long and tie the two ends together. Place the outstretched string on the ground in a chosen spot. The string marks the boundaries of the investigation. What can be found within that area? Are there any minibeasts and if so what type? Count them. Explore it minutely. A magnifying glass can help to see small items. List them down. Look at any tracks, footprints or marks and work out who might have made them.

Comparisons with sections in other areas can throw up some interesting findings. Are the same types of mini beasts to be found in both or are there more of one species than another? If soil can be seen – is it the same colour?

Bush bugs

Take: A white cloth – the larger the better. A bug box and magnifying glasses are useful, but not essential

Choose a bush with plenty of leaves on it, and if possible flowers or berries. Place the cloth underneath and gently shake a branch over the cloth. Any insects present on the branch will fall onto the cloth and can be seen easily. Try comparing what falls out of different branches, or branches with leaves but not flowers, or just from the flowers. Look for the presence of glossy green shield bugs, flies, beetles, ladybirds, and caterpillars.

A word of warning – before shaking a branch with flowers on, make sure there are no bees or wasps in it.

When the children have finished investigating the various insects, gently lift the cloth and place the insects back into the bush.

Conkers

Take: String, skewer
Find: Conkers

This game can only be played in the autumn. Look for horse chestnut trees. These are easily identified by their large leaves and seed cases covered with spikes. Look for spiny seed cases on the ground which have broken open to reveal a hard, brown seed inside. These can be collected and taken home.

Conker games

Use a skewer to pierce a hole right through the conker. It is not easy and requires a lot of effort. Push a piece of string through the conker, tying a knot at one end to secure the conker in place. Holding the string, try to hit your opponent's conker with yours. Take care not to hit each other. The aim is to try and break your opponent's conker.

Catch a falling leaf

A blustery autumn day and leaves falling from the trees can create a lot of fun for children. As they walk along, encourage them to try and catch a leaf as it falls to the ground. This is not as easy as it sounds since the leaves do not fall straight! Legend has it that catching a falling leaf will bring you good luck in the year to come. Who knows? But it certainly is fun to try!

Daisy chains

Find: Daisies

Daisy chain making is a very relaxing activity which little girls especially really enjoy. All you need are some daisies. Make sure that the daisies have fairly long stems. Using your nails, gently pierce a slit in a daisy stem. Thread another daisy stem through this slit. Then make a slit in the next daisy stem, thread a daisy through and so on. This can go on as long as you want, creating a long chain or small circle by joining just three or four daisies together. Once complete they can be used as bracelets, necklaces or as decoration.

Dandelion clocks

Find: a dandelion that has gone to seed

Children enjoy the fun of blowing the dandelion seeds away. Pick a dandelion, which no longer has any petals left and is just a mass of seed. Blow gently and see how many times you have to blow before all the seeds have gone. This is sometimes used as a fun way to tell the time. The number of times you have to blow to remove all the seeds, is said to indicate how many hours have passed.

Decidious v evergreen

Can you identify easily which is deciduous and which is evergreen? This activity can be undertaken throughout the year identifying the differences in texture and colour. Why do some trees lose their leaves in winter? Why do others keep them? What makes the leaves different? Look for the waxy coating on evergreen leaves and compare this to the texture of leaves belonging to deciduous trees. Explore how the colours and textures of the leaves of deciduous trees changes in the autumn.

Dragon breath

A very simple yet entertaining activity which livens up, walks on a frosty, cold day. The cold air freezes your breath as you breathe out making it look like smoke. Try breathing out in different ways – what shape does a long breathe make? What shape does a series of short breaths make? Can you make a long continuous plume? Can you make it circle around? Which would be most like dragon breath?

Dusk or dawn walks

Try going for a walk at dusk rather than during the daytime. The world seems a very different place as night begins to fall. Listen to the bird song – it is always very noticeable at night. How many different songs can be heard? What shadows are cast by trees, or yourselves as you walk along? Is it eerie or exciting? Listen out for the sound of bats and owls as they hunt in the evening sky.

Dawn walks do require getting up very early – but it can be worth it. Children see the world in very different light as they see the sun rise in the sky. Who can hear the first bird? Listen to the dawn chorus that erupts as birds wake up. How much busier is it at the end of the walk compared to when you started?

Find out the age of a hedge

If you know there is a well-established hedge to be found on your walk, this can be a good activity to get kids thinking.

Take: A piece of card with a long strip of double sided sticky tape along one edge
Find: 2 sticks

Place one stick on the ground near the hedge. Walk 40 long steps alongside the hedge then lay down the second stick. Looking only at the section of hedge between the two sticks, take a leaf from each type of shrub you find. Only count each type of shrub or tree once. Place the leaf on the sticky tape. Check all new leaves against the ones already on the card to make sure they are different.

Use only leaves from plants with woody stems. These are shrubs or trees. Do not include any plants with soft stems such as buttercups or daisies.

When all the leaves have been collected, count up how many leaves you have on your card. This will tell you the rough age of the hedge.

For every different kind of shrub the hedge is approximately one hundred years old.

This activity can be repeated using hedges in different locations. Which hedge is the oldest? Which is the youngest?

Flint knapping

Take: Safety goggles
Find: A large pebble to use as a hammer

Flint knapping is an old traditional technique that dates back to Neolithic times. It is can be undertaken anywhere flints can be found. Flints are shards of rock that can be chipped to make sharp points. Neolithic people used flint to make arrowheads, axes and spear heads. The biggest concentration of flint is to be found in East Anglia.

This is a particularly suitable for older children, although younger ones can try it as long as they are carefully supervised. There is a risk of injury. It is easy to miss the flint and hit yourself with the stone. Sharp pieces can cut, and when flint knapping small pieces can fly up into the face. Wearing safety goggles to protect the eyes is a good idea.

To knap flint you will need a piece of flint and a large stone. The stone should fit comfortably into the palm of the hand. Sit down and take the piece of flint into one hand. Using the pebble in your other hand, carefully chip off shards around the edge. Do not try to break too much off too quickly. The exact size and shape of the shards will depend on the angle at which the flint is hit. Aim to work evenly around the edge of the flint, carefully shaping it.

Look at the shards that have broken off the large piece of flint. Some of these may be easier to chip into shape. Triangular shaped pieces can be turned into arrowheads.

You will need to experiment to find what suits you best. This is a task, which requires patience. It takes time and effort to knap flints. Flint knapping is not something that can be rushed. Always remember that flint is very sharp and can cut.

Foraging

Take: Containers to hold food, a book to identify wild food

In a world dominated by supermarkets and fast food, there has been a decrease in interest in wild food. Yet people for centuries have gathered food from the wild; it is free and very nutritious. Children love the idea of gathering something from nature and then being able to eat it, so why not look out for suitable food on your walks?

Always remember that there are poisonous berries and plants. Be sure of your identification before eating. If you are hesitant about what to pick and use, there are lots of books in libraries that can give you the information you need.

Nut

Sweet chestnut

Sloe

Blackberry

Field Mushroom

Wild food

Avoid gathering berries and other food close to busy roads. Concentrate on woods, quiet roads, hedges and open countryside.

Many plants are easily identifiable. The most common are:

Bilberries – these are found mainly in upland areas. The bushes are small and the fruit is hidden among the leaves but it is worth the effort.

Blackberries - in late summer and autumn, bramble patches in woods and hedgerows are full of delicious blackberries. They might stain the hands but they are lovely to eat fresh as well as taking home to make pies and jam, or simply freeze for future use.

Elderberries – the juicy black berries can be turned into a delicious cordial. In the spring, the lacy white flowers can be eaten.

Rose hips – gather the hips, remove the seeds and turn the remainder into soft pulpy syrup – this contains more vitamin C than oranges. Beware – the seeds are covered in tiny hairs, which make a very effective itching powder!!!

Sloes – these should only be collected after the first frosts and when they are really black. Sloes can be turned into a lovely jelly.

Fungi – found everywhere in woods and fields in autumn. Do NOT pick and use unless you are absolutely certain as to identification. Many varieties can be poisonous and can kill or make you very ill.

If you want to forage for fungi it is best to go on an organized fungi walk led by a specialist. Details of such walks can be easily found by looking in local newspapers, or by contacting organisations such as Wildlife Trusts. The specialist will ensure the walk covers an area where fungi can be found and will carefully check all that is found to make sure that it is safe to touch and eat. Take a basket with you to collect your fungi.

Hazelnuts – roast lightly and then shell them.

Marjoram – this is a common summer flowering plant found in chalk country. Gather the leaves before the flowers open and use as an addition to meals. Alternatively place the leaves on a baking tray and place in a cool oven to dry. When crumbly, place in a jar for winter use.

Raspberries – wild raspberries can be found in woods and countryside. Usually slightly smaller than modern garden versions they are very sweet.

Stinging nettles – no, this is not a joke – they are a traditional food and are very nutritious being full of vitamins. Wear gloves when gathering them. Take only the young tops of the plant. These can be cooked in water and pureed to make a soup. Alternatively pour hot water onto a few leaves and leave to brew. This makes a refreshing herbal tea. The longer you leave the leaves in the water, the stronger the tea.

Strawberries wild strawberries are small but intensely sweet. These can be found almost anywhere.

Sweet Chestnuts – found in autumn underneath chestnut trees. Remove the spiky green shells and the sweet nuts inside can be eaten.

Wild mint – run your fingers through the leaves – the smell is instantly identifiable. Collect leaves for drying or cooking, or use to make mint tea.

Some basic do's and don't when foraging

- Have a plant identification book to hand
- Go on an expert walk to collect fungi. There are always lots of organised fungi walks in autumn
- Never eat anything about which you are not certain.
- Only take food growing away from main roads. Anything growing on roadside bushes is likely to be polluted by exhaust fumes
- Do not trample or damage other plants when picking wild food
- Never pick more than you absolutely need
- Only harvest wild food in areas that are open to the public. Do not trespass on private land.

Grass collecting

Take: A field guide to grasses

Grass is grass – or is it? A close investigation will reveal many differences. The grass leaves may be soft or shiny, thin or wide. When flowering, the seed heads can be all kinds of sizes, shapes and even different colours. Some grass is sticky to the touch, and seed heads can stick to clothing. Some seed heads are very fine and delicate, others are chunky and come off easily as you slide your fingers upwards. Some are sweet to suck, while others can make an ear splitting noise when you blow across the leaves. Beware – some grasses can be very sharp and can cut fingers just like a paper cut.

How many different types can you find? This can become very competitive if more than one child is involved. Children can get very enthusiastic and keen to get the highest number of varieties.

At home, the seed heads can be fastened to paper as a display or made into a collage.

Try sowing some of the seeds in a pot and see what will grow.

Growing trees

In the autumn, collect acorns, conkers, and ash or sycamore seeds and put them in small pots. Empty yoghurt pots work quite well for this purpose. Fill with a little compost, add the seed, cover and leave in a cool place. The seeds need a period of cold in which to encourage germination.

See how many seedling trees appear. The young trees can be repotted into a larger pot and kept there for around two years. After this they do need to be planted out. Remember

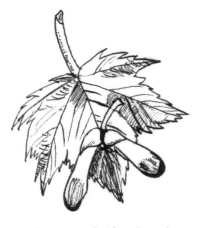

Sycamore leaf and seed

they will grow tall, so unless you have plenty of space don't plant them out in the garden. Instead give them to nature groups such as Woodland Trust or see if your local community has a tree officer who can arrange for them to be planted in your neighbourhood.

Helicopters

Find: Seeds from an ash or sycamore tree

This is very much an autumn activity which children can do as they walk along, or play while having a break. Look for the twirling seeds of ash or sycamore trees. Collect some. Throw them into the air and watch them spiral down, turning just like helicopter wings. Have a competition – whose wings reach the ground first?

Leaf piles

Find: Dry leaves

Dry weather is essential. This activity only works when the leaves are dry and crisp.

Choose an area where there has been a heavy leaf fall. Collect up as many leaves as possible into a big pile. Then, let the children jump into it and throw armfuls of leaves at each other. Just walking in the pile and kicking up the leaves gives lots of fun. This can get very lively so take special care if there are very young children involved.

Alternatively encourage the children to take turns climbing to the top of the pile, then sliding down as the leaves scatter around them.

Leaf study

Take: A magnifying glass
Find: Some leaves

An autumn activity encouraging children to look closely at leaves. Encourage children to look for two very special leaves as they walk. The reasons for choosing the leaves can vary from walk to walk. It could be the two largest leaves they can find, the two most colourful leaves, or the two smallest leaves, or just simply the two leaves that appeal to them most.

When they have found the leaves, let them sit down and explain why they have chosen those particular leaves. What appeals to them about the leaves? Why did they make that particular choice? What else can they see about the leaves? Are there any insects living on the leaf? Are there any holes or any indication that the leaf has been nibbled by caterpillars?

This activity encourages close concentrated study of the leaf, and is good for vocabulary development.

When everyone has finished talking about their leaf, tell them to turn around so that their backs are to the leaves. Collect up all the leaves and mix them up. Then spread them out on the ground again. At this point everyone can turn round. Their task is then quite simple – can you find your special leaf again?

Listen to a tree's heartbeat

Take: A stethoscope

This activity is most effective in spring or autumn as it enables you to hear the sap moving within a tree. In Spring, the sap rises quite quickly up a tree; while in autumn it can heard moving downwards. Choose a young tree with a thin bark. Silver Birch trees are perfect for this exercise if you can find any in your locality. Put the stethoscope against the side of the tree and listen carefully. The stethoscope may need to be moved around a few times until you find the right spot. You should be able to hear a soft running sound, a bit like water in a small stream. Sometimes putting an ear directly against the bark will allow you to hear the sap rising or falling, but this does require very good hearing.

Log balancing

Quick and easy to do. Look for some large tree trunks lying along the path. Can the children walk along them without falling off? Younger children will need a helping hand to keep their balance. It is just like walking a tightrope.

Map reading

Take: A map of the proposed walk area

If children have never read a map before, start with simple ones found in country parks where walks are marked with arrows and colours.

Let the children organise the walk. Using the map, they decide on the route to follow and then they try to match the map's instructions with what they are seeing as they walk. Can they follow the right trail? You will need to keep a close eye on their choices, so that if they go off course, they can be quickly set right.

Map and compass

This is an activity, which is good for developing a child's self-confidence, encouraging them to navigate around strange areas. As they become more skilled at following a map, you can introduce them to maps from books about walks or Ordnance Survey maps. They will need to learn all the symbols beforehand, so practise creating some outline walks at home before actually going off on a walk with a map.

Make a den

Find: Fallen branches, leaves

Children enjoy creating dens. It is a good activity for an area in which you go for regular walks. Children like going back time and time again to the site of a den. Look for a suitable spot ideally about half to three quarters of the way along a route you use frequently. This gives them something to look forward to as they walk along. Building a den involves creating a simple shelter. It can be created among tree roots overshadowed by low branches or among a group of bushes.

Once the den is made, allow time for the children to play or have a picnic before moving on. When they next return, they can make improvements to the den, tidy it up, rebuild or just use it as a play area for a while.

When building a den:

- Avoid causing too much disturbance to the woodland, birds and animals

- Make sure there are lots of dead wood, leaves and branches around which can be used in the building process

- Use a natural feature wherever possible as the basis for the den such as overhanging branches

- Do not use materials possessing thorns or prickles

There are many different ways to actually build a den or woodland shelter. Among the most common ways are:

- Prop tall, thin sticks on either side of an overhanging tree branch. Use bracken, dead leaves and other materials to cover the sides

- Make a tepee style den by propping long branches around the sides of a tree. Cover the sides with natural materials

- Use a gap between two trees. Fill in the gap with a framework of branches and a covering of bracken

- Use three fallen branches tied tightly together with natural fibres such as honeysuckle or ivy. Wedge these against a fallen log, then add other branches to form sides. Do not make this type of construction too high otherwise it may become unsafe

- Weaving smaller twigs and thinner branches through the basic framework to create a lattice can also create the sides of a den. This can then be used to support a covering of leaves, grasses and bracken.

Making nettle rope

Take: Scissors or secateurs to cut the nettles, a knife, strong gloves
Find: A patch of stinging nettles

This can be a painful activity if you are not careful, but it is worth trying. Children are always surprised by how strong and easy it is to create rope from stinging nettles. It takes some time and patience – you need to allow at least half an hour for this activity.

Cut some nettles and strip off the stinging leaves. It is then safe to remove your gloves. Using the knife carefully cut the stem in half lengthways. This will expose the inner pith. Peel the pith away leaving the green exterior stem. Fasten at least three stems together with a knot at the top. Then carefully twist or plait the stems together. To make a strong rope, the plaiting or twisting must be done as tightly as possible. The resultant rope is thin, but strong. It can be made even stronger by plaiting several thin ropes together.

Making a peashooter

Take: A knife
Find: A piece of elder stem, a sharp twig

For generations, children have used elder wood to make peashooters. You need a piece of elder that is around 3cm/1 inch in diameter. Cut a section measuring no longer than 20cm/8 inches long. It is best to experiment on smaller versions as these are easiest to make.

Having obtained your piece of stem, look for a hard twig. The twig should be roughly the same diameter as the pithy core of the elder stem. Use the twig to dig out the pithy core. You may need to sharpen the twig using a knife. The pith can be dug out from both ends of the stem. Continue until all the pith has been removed and there is a clear tube from top to bottom. Slip a pea into the top of the tube and then blow hard. If you have made the peashooter correctly, it will fire the pea out of the other end at some speed.

Never fire the peashooter towards people, animals or birds. Being on the receiving end can hurt. Far better to have a game and discover what is the longest distance a pea can be blown. Competitions of this kind immediately gain the attention of any child. Alternatively, indicate a target, such as a tree trunk or log and see who can hit it by blowing a pea from their peashooter.

Making a whistle

Take: A knife
Find: A piece of elder stem, a sharp twig

Elder stems also make good simple whistles. Choose a piece of elder stem that is not more than 3cm/1 inch in diameter. Cut a small section. Using a sharp twig, gently dig out the pithy core. This can be done from both ends. When all the pith is removed, you should have a smooth tube. Pierce a hole in one side of the tube. Blowing down the tube and lifting a finger on and off the hole will create different sounds.

Experiment with different sized tubes. Does the sound vary? Which makes the highest sound? Which makes the lowest sound?

Try putting more holes in the tube and playing it like a recorder. What difference does this make to the variety of sounds that can be made?

Minibeast hunting

Take: Magnifying glass, bug boxes, old paintbrushes

Giving a child a magnifying glass can open up a whole new world and add lots of interest to a walk. It doesn't matter where you are walking – along bridle paths, churchyards, foot paths, disused railway lines, through woods or fields, a child with a magnifying glass will find something new each time. Each type of habitat will

Looking for minibeasts is great fun. Look for logs that can be easily rolled over to reveal centipedes, millipedes, beetles, slow worms, worms, woodlice, earwigs, and other tiny creatures. They may also be found under piles of leaves, stones or in crevices among the trees. All logs, stones and other materials should be replaced exactly as they were when you have finished looking in the area.

Old paintbrushes will allow you to gently brush insects into bug boxes that have integral magnifying glasses. Always remember to remove any insects collected in this way and replace them where they were found.

If a child becomes really keen on finding out more about minibeasts, there are many field guides available which enable the minibeasts to be identified.

Minibeasts

Moths

Take: White sheet, pillowcase or tea towel, torch, treacle, jam or golden syrup

This activity is an ideal accompaniment to a dusk walk during spring and summer. It can only be done at dusk as this is when the moths appear. They can be very beautiful possessing intricate markings.

Look for a clearing, open area or meadow edge where you can wait for a little while. Hang the white material from a tree branch or similar tall object. Shine a bright torch onto the material and wait. The bigger the torch lens the better when attracting moths. Moths will be attracted to the light, but can fly off safely whenever they wish.

Try moving the white material to other places. Do the same type of moths appear or are they different?

Alternatively smear some treacle, jam or golden syrup onto the side of a tree. Moths will be attracted to the sweet liquid and will come to feed. Watch them using the light of a torch.

Night walks

Take: Torches with red cellophane over the lens

This adds a very different dimension to any walk. Not many people go for a walk once it is dark. The sheer excitement of being out at night can encourage children to go much further than they expect. Wrap up warmly as it can get chilly quite quickly at this time. Make sure you know the route very well – it is easy to get lost or loose your sense of direction at night. It can help to choose a route familiar to the children – they will know where they are going, but see it from a very different viewpoint.

Walking when it is really dark through a wood or across a field offers a very different experience. Keep torches pointing downwards to illuminate any obstacles along the path. If possible, place red cellophane over the lens. This will reduce glare. Move as quietly as possible so that you can listen to the noises made by animals moving through the bushes, the cries of foxes and owls. How many can you identify? Remember that even a whisper can carry a long way.

Find a clearing and stop. Turn out all the torches and stay very still. It will take a few minutes for your eyes to get used to the total dark, but you will find that you can still see a lot. Look up at the sky – how many stars are there? Careful observation may reveal the shapes of the great bear (Ursus major) or constellations such as the Archer. What shape is the moon? This is a good way for children to learn about the night sky, and the changing shapes of the moon. It also helps them to begin to understand the problem posed by lights. All too frequently, much of the night sky is lit up by lights from towns and roads. When in town, it can be very hard to actually see the night sky. Viewed from a country area, the towns are clearly highlighted at night.

As your night vision improves, you will start to see other objects around you such as the pale bark of birch trees, the outlines of bushes and trees. Listen carefully – what can you hear?

With good night vision, and patiently staying very still, it may be possible to glimpse animals moving through bushes or along tracks. Glow worms can occasionally be spotted crawling on the ground. This is a magical sight that is not often seen.

Look for a fallen tree branch, stone or log that can be easily rolled over. How many mini-beasts are active at night? Remember to replace the stone or log just as you found it when you have finished.

Similar exercises can be undertaken on any open spot such as grassland or in the countryside. But it must be in an area which is not affected by modern day lighting, or even car headlights.

When undertaking a night walk it is very important to ensure:

- Everyone has to stay close together
- Children should walk very carefully
- An adult should be at the front and the rear of the group
- Children holding candle lanterns must be carefully supervised.

Orienteering

Take: An easy to follow map

Some preparation is needed beforehand. Choose a walk with which you are familiar. Create a simple map showing key points that can be found such as a church tower, a very tall tree in the middle of a field, a stream, a bridge, a stile. Label each point on the map. The aim is for the child to follow the map and find each labelled point in the order you have specified.

Puddle splashing

Take: Rubber boots

This is a fun activity for a rainy day or when the rain has stopped. Children love splashing through the puddles, kicking up the water and watching if fall back to the ground.

Try varying the way in which they splash through the puddles. Can they jump from puddle to puddle? Perhaps there is

Jumping in the puddles

a monster in the way, and they have to escape it by reaching the next puddle. Can they jump lightly without causing much of a splash so that they do not alert the monster? Or are they planning to soak the monster?

Young children could pretend they are ducks swimming in a pond, making swimming motions with their arms. Several young children could try following in a line just like ducklings follow the mother duck.

This activity can get very messy. Puddles can be muddy so be prepared to clean up children afterwards!

Rain catching

Take: A small lidless container

Very few children enjoy walking in the rain, especially when it starts to get heavy. Encouraging them to walk that bit faster so as to find shelter, and distracting them from complaints about getting wet and uncomfortable becomes a priority.

When the first drops of rain begin, children can try catching raindrops as they fall. Hardest of all is when they try and catch the raindrops on their tongues!

As rain gets heavier or drizzle sets in, try giving each child a small lidless container to catch the rain in. When they get home, they can measure how much rain is in the container. Who has collected the most rain?

Rushes

When walking through damp, wet areas look out for clumps of green rushes. These grow about 12 to 18 inches high and are bright green in colour, with thin, bendy stems. Pluck a stem as you walk and try to peel off the outer covering revealing white pith inside. This can be done using your nails. If done carefully, the whole stem comes away. Traditionally the pith was used to make rush lights which when slowly burnt gave off a small light.

Sticky grass

Look for sticky grass on your travels. Then liven up a few minutes of the walk with a sticky grass battle. Pulled apart and thrown gently, it will stick to clothes!

Stories

Take: Some background research on local stories and legends

Before going out on a walk, check out the area through which you are walking for local stories and legends. There may even be ghost stories! Local libraries usually have a good selection of local books if you are new to an area.

Tell the stories as you walk. Listening to the stories will keep children's attention. Typical stories could include the tale of the Peddler of Swaffham while walking on the Peddlers Way, the Pancake Witch sizzling pancakes under Conger Hill in Bedfordshire or tales of Robin Hood while exploring the tracks through Sherwood Forest.

Almost every area has a wide range of fun stories and local legends which are guaranteed to enthral a child. Who could resist tales of the Black Dog chasing through the church at Bungay in Suffolk or leaving its claw marks on the church door at Blythburgh!

Sweep netting

Take: A sweep net, magnifying glasses and bug boxes are useful but not essential

This is an activity, which require a little bit of preparation beforehand. Sweep nets are easily made by taking an old pillowcase and cutting it in half. Keep the bottom half and discard the half with the opening. Sew a hem round the edge, leaving part unsown. Push a piece of bendy wire – garden wire will do – through the hem and fasten in place. The wire will enable the pillowcase to stay open.

To use a sweep net, find an area of tall grass. Hold one side of the rim of the net with both hands. Keeping the net at right angles to the ground, gently swing the net from side to side in an arc as you walk along. After a short while, stop and have a look at what is inside.

Use a bug box or magnifying glass to look closely at any insects. When you have finished looking, gently turn the net inside out to release any insects back into the grass.

Try doing a comparison in different areas. Are the same type of insects being found? Are more insects present if there are wild flowers in the area?

Tree climbing

Every child loves climbing trees so why not encourage it to have a go? This can be done in a clearing, or along the path during the walk. It encourages agility as well as physical development.

When climbing trees, look for trees that have clear handholds at a height that a child can reach. Particularly suitable are trees that have a divided trunk offering a secure foothold and large, thick branches. Older trees tend to be best.

Obviously there are some dangers and clear rules on what is allowed should be set beforehand.

Climbing high

- Clearly indicate how high children are allowed to climb. It should be a height with which you, as a parent or guardian, are comfortable. If they suddenly get scared or need help you should be able to reach them easily

- Choose a mature tree with strong branches
- There should be no more than one child to a branch at any one time
- All branches should be tested before stepping on them
- Children should first check branches for any obvious splits or breaks
- No climbing on dead branches
- Children should stay close to the trunk of the tree – this is the safest area
- Any nests found while climbing a tree should not be disturbed
- Check the base of the tree to ensure there are no sharp edges, broken bottles or other rubbish that could cause harm when landing
- Do not attempt to climb trees when it is windy or the bark is slippery.

Tree top study

Take: A small mirror. Ideally one mirror for each child is needed

It is easy to see what is around you when you are walking among trees – but trees are much more than that. There is a whole new world to be found at tree top level. Using a mirror helps see much higher than eye level. Angle the mirror so that it gives a view of the tops of trees. It takes a bit of time and effort to get it right as it varies according to the height of the user. It works best if the mirror is held just below the eyes.

Look out for birds taking flight and see if you can spot any bird's nests or squirrel's drey's. You might see a squirrel leaping around the tops of trees, or bird's landing within them. Look too at the shape of the top of the tree – what is it like? Is it dense, or thin? Spiky or broad? Do the branches look thin or thick? Quite detailed discussions can result.

This activity can be repeated in different places and with different trees. Each experience will be different as no two trees are the same. Autumn is one of the best times of the year to try this activity due to the varied leaf colour, but it is something that can be undertaken at any time of the year. It will always reveal something different.

Also try putting the several mirrors together on the floor of the forest and looking into them. Be careful not to block the view! This gives the impression of a pool of mirrors reflecting the sky.

Waking the senses

Ideal for younger children, the aim is to encourage them to focus on just one sense at a time. As you walk, encourage them to look and see what they can find.

Then change the focus. Cover the child's eyes with a blindfold and either guide them along the path, or stop in a convenient place for a few minutes. There should be no talking, just listening. Then find out what they can hear.

Remove the blindfold and go a bit further. What can they feel? This can be played as you walk along. Encourage them to touch different objects such as tree bark, a shiny leaf, and a stone. What do they feel like? Is it soft, hard, slippery, slimy?

Try blindfolding the child before giving them a selection of natural objects. Let them feel the objects, then tell you what it is. Are they right or wrong?

What can you find in a hedge?

This requires careful hunting and looking. The closer they look, the more that can be found.

Things to look for include:

Nests
Rubbish
Seeds
Nuts
Deciduous plants
Evergreen plants
Flowers
Animals
Minibeasts

Insects
Berries
Fungi (depending on the time of the year)

If there is more than one child, give them each a different part of the hedge to concentrate on. Laying down sticks on the ground to identify specific areas or using natural features such as the area between two trees can do this. Compare findings. What differences and similarities can be found? Which is the busiest part of the hedge?

Geocaching

Take: Hand held GPS system (a mobile phone may include one)

Ideal for older kids, this is a challenging game of hiding and seeking treasure and is a great way to encourage kids to explore the outdoors.

The idea is to find a specific site using only GPS co-ordinates. To find sites in your area you have to register for free basic membership at www.geocaching.com. Then you click on 'Hide and Seek a Cache' and enter your postal code. This will tell you where the nearest cache is located in your area. Go to the location and then follow the instructions which appear on the GPS device. Arrows may point the way, and other co-ordinates may be given. When you get to the next location, you may be instructed to go to another spot. When you eventually find the cache, you sign the log book and return it to its original location. Anyone can set up a cache with instructions for others to follow.

A variation on this system exists in South Norfolk where the local council has set up a cache trail. Participants can hire a GPS system from a leisure centre and follow specially designed cache trails at locations in commons and woods across the area. Some walks are easier than others, and can last between 10 minutes and 90 minutes.

Seaside and waterside activities

Walking beside along the shore or other watery environments can offer very special opportunities for games and activities to keep children interested. Generally these require little extra equipment beyond what you can find as you walk. From simple boat building to erosion, skimming stones to playing Canute there is something for all ages. Consider too the many games and activities listed earlier in this book – many of these can easily be adapted to suit this environment. Take Alien for example – children could be asked to find objects that are alien to a riverside setting.

Safety considerations are essential. Children should never be left unsupervised near water. Young children can fall and drown in just a few inches of water. Keep an eye on what they are doing. On beaches, remember that the tide can come in very quickly. Every year, there are tales of children and adults being swept away by the sea, having ventured out too far when the tide is about to turn.

Boat making

Find: Natural materials

This is a fun activity for use alongside any source of water. Use any natural materials at hand such as feathers, pieces of bark, leaves, shells, acorn cases, and reeds. Pierce leaves with a light twig to make

Ahoy there!

a sail, and put the twig into a seed case, held in place by bits of moss or grass. Feathers also make good sails. Reeds can be woven together to make a miniature boat or raft. A piece of bark can be pierced by a feather to make a simple boat. Make several boats and race them down the stream? Whose boat reaches a chosen spot first? Can they find their way past rocks and other obstacles in their way? How quickly will the boat travel? Will it be sent to one side or other of the stream? Which materials work best?

Canute

Find: Stones

Can you build a structure that will stand up the power of the sea? Build stone towers or small castles along the edge of the shoreline just as the tide is turning. Watch to see which tower withstands the power of the sea for the longest period, and which tower falls first.

Canal art

Take: Paper and pencils

When walking along rivers and canals, look out for canal boats. Many will be brightly decorated with detailed pictures of castles, roses, boating scenes. Colours are always bright and eye-catching. What examples can you see? Draw some of the styles that appeal most. On returning home, try to create your own canal art. Decorate a

Canal art roses

flowerpot or box. Use typical canal art colours such as reds, yellows and whites.

Environmental art

Take: Camera
Find: Natural materials

This is ephemeral art, which returns naturally to the environment in due course. Only natural materials native to the area are used such as pebbles, sand, twigs, driftwood, seaweed, and shells. Gather up suitable materials and then create your own sculpture or picture on the ground. Art creations can be anything, for example: a scene, a comment on the way people leave the environment, a mythical creature, a shell or a person. Once complete, take a picture of it to remind you of what you have done, then leave it for other people to see and admire before it breaks down naturally with the weather.

Erosion

Take: Bucket and spade

Build a small village of sand houses, complete with roads. Fill a container with water. Approaching the sand village from the front, try to tip the water against the houses just like sea waves hitting the coast. How long do the houses stay in place? Do smaller waves have more or less effect than stormy ones?

Repeat the exercise using houses made of stones. Which lasts longer against the 'waves?'

This is a good exercise to help children understand the power of the sea and how it slowly erodes the coastline.

How many?

This is best undertaken in an area with which you are familiar. Think of something you know occurs frequently – it might be shells, crabs or pebbles with holes inside. Alternatively you could choose colours as a theme, eg: 12 items that are yellow. Set a time limit or a distance. How many of the specified items can be found in that time or distance? This can get quite competitive if more than one child is involved, so a referee may be needed!

Night time seashore walks

Take: Torches, candle, night lights

These walks need to be organised very carefully. Make sure you are fully aware of any tide changes and do not walk too close to the sea itself. Walking at night along the seashore is a magical activity and introduces a child to a whole new world. Keep torches pointing downwards, and cover the lenses with red cellophane. Eyes quickly become accustomed to the night. Listen to the sound of the sea – it can sound much louder at night. You may even see it faintly glowing depending on the amount of phosphorescent present.

Rock pools can offer the opportunity for an unusual boat building activity. Use a small piece of driftwood or plastic washed up on the beach. Add a night-light and let it sail on the pool. Always remember to remove all non-natural objects afterwards.

Take care:

- Do not walk along the beach when the tide is coming in
- Do not walk on the beach at night if there is any risk of quicksand
- Do not go too close to the water
- Children should stay close to the adults
- Make sure you cannot be caught by incoming tides
- Remember that tides can come in faster than you expect.

Pooh sticks

Find: Sticks

Winnie the Pooh first discovered the game of Pooh Sticks when he dropped a pine cone over one side of a bridge and then discovered it re-appeared on the other side. After this, Winnie the Pooh and his friends spent many hours dropping sticks from one side of a bridge and seeing whose stick appeared first on the other side.

Playing Pooh sticks

Children love playing this game whenever they come to a bridge. All that is needed are a few sticks, large leaves, feathers or any other natural material that will float. Begin by working out which way the stream or river is flowing. Drop a stick over the upstream side of the bridge and then run to the downstream side of the bridge and watch it reappear. Does it come quickly or slowly? Much will depend on the strength of the current. What is the effect if the stick is dropped in a slightly different spot?

Sand sculptures

Take: Bucket and spade, camera

This is best undertaken with wet sand. Build up the sand to create a three dimensional sculpture such as a crab, fish or boat. Take a photo to remind you of your design, then leave it for others to enjoy.

Sea monsters

As you walk, look for natural features that suggest eyes, mouth, hair, fins, wings or even arms and legs. It could be a group of stones or boulders, cracks in the cliff face, or bulges in the sand. Having spied something, use natural materials around you such as seaweed, shells, and stones to bring the monster to life. If eyes have been found, add some hair and fins; or wings and a long snout. Why not make up a story about the monster?

The sea monster

Seaweed fun

Find: Seaweed

Look for bladder wrack along the strand line. This is deep green and has raised pockets of air along its length. Children will be kept amused as they 'pop' the pockets of air. Who can make the loudest pop?

Skimming

Find: Flat, lightweight stones

Older children usually find this easier than younger ones. It does require lots of practice.

The aim is to skim stones across the water so that they skip one or more times before finally sinking. The stone has to be flat and lightweight. It should not be too small or too large. If it is too heavy, it will sink immediately. Hold the stone between the fingers. Aim at a 45° degree angle to the water, and throw the stone. With luck it should skim over the surface, touching the water once or twice before sinking.

The aim is to make a stone skim over the surface of the water as many times as possible and to go as far as it can before finally losing impetus and sinking. The technique requires practise and care. Do not throw in an under or over arm motion as this will cause the stone to sink immediately.

Imagine throwing a Frisbee – the same technique is needed. The back end of the stone should be held by the index finger with the front of the stone resting on the tip of the middle finger and held down by the thumb. Draw the arm back until fully extended then move the arm quickly forwards in a horizontal direction for about a quarter of a circle aiming at the water. Let go. The stone should by then have enough force to shoot forwards and skim over the surface.

Skittles

Find: Lots of pebbles

This game can be played anywhere you can find a good selection of stones, such as pebble beaches, edges of lakes and rivers.

Build a stone tower. Gather a selection of smaller sized pebbles. Standing or sitting at an agreed distance from the tower, each person takes a turn throwing a pebble at the tower. Who can hit it? Who succeeds in knocking it down? This is a game that can become quite addictive with everyone wanting to prove they are the better shot.

Take care to ensure that stones are not thrown if people are near the target; or at each other.

Shell mosaics

Find: Lots of shells

Lay the shells out on the sand to form a mosaic picture. This can take a few minutes or half an hour depending on the creativity of the children. Encourage them to use different shaped shells and see how they can be fitted together.

Strand line surveys

This is a useful activity that can keep children moving steadily along a beach. Walk at the strand line – that is the furthest limit of the tide on a beach. See what the tide has brought in. This is often where starfish can be found, unusual shells, sea glass, crabs and mermaids purses. Keeping eyes peeled carefully can result in some amazing finds.

Stone castles

Find: Stones

Collect stones and build them into castles. They can be given extra stability by adding driftwood into the construction. Look for stones that have a flattish base. Use large stones as the base, adding smaller stones as the structure grows.

On guard in the castle

Stone mobiles

Take: Some string
Find: Stones which have a hole through them

This is an activity that can take some time. Look for stones that have a hole through them. These holes have been made naturally by the process of erosion and by sea creatures boring through the stone. Tie a knot in one end of the string and thread the stones onto it. This will create an unusual mobile, which can be hung up on a tree when you get home.

Stone towers

Find: Lots of pebbles

Pebble beaches have their own fascination. Try building towers out of pebbles. Look for large pebbles with flattish sides. Place them one on another and see how big a tower you can build.

A lot of care is needed – one wrong stone and the entire tower can come toppling down.

Water dipping

Take: A small fishing net, a plastic tray or container, a guidebook about water creatures can be helpful

This can be undertaken in any watery environment – sea, pond, rock pool, river or lake. Avoid areas that are polluted, muddy or have been recently disturbed.

Choose a spot where the child can reach safely into the water. It should not be too deep. Dip the plastic container into the water so that it is half full. Place the container on the ground nearby. Using the fishing net, draw a figure of eight below the surface of the water. Pull to the surface and gently tip any contents into the container. If nothing has been caught, try again in the same or a different spot. In rivers and ponds, it is worth trying near reeds or shady areas. See how many creatures you can catch and identify.

When the tray is full or you are ready to leave, gently pour the contents back into the water.

Do not handle any creatures with your hands as you can accidentally hurt the creatures. There may also be creatures in the net that can hurt you such as jellyfish.

This is an activity that can be undertaken several times a year in the same area. Different creatures will be found each time and can include anything from water beetles, dragonfly larvae to fish and flies.

Waste sculptures

Find: Natural materials

Look for waste materials that have been left on the beach or by the river. Typical items include driftwood, tin cans, plastic bottles, rope. Look carefully at them and see if they can be turned into a sculpture of some kind. Some plastic bottles might make the body of an octopus while rope could form its tentacles.

Always check rubbish first before allowing children to use it. Make sure it is not contaminated by oil or possesses rough edges that could cause harm.

Leave the sculptures in place for other people to see.

Wave fun

Take: An orange or an apple

At first sight it always looks as though tides come in and go out in a straight line, but in reality tide direction can vary hugely. Individual waves can go out at 45° to the shore. Try and work out which direction they think the waves are moving. Then see who is right by throwing an orange or apple into the sea and watch how it comes in and out again with the tide. Within a short time, the fruit will end up quite a long way from where it started.

What can you find?

Choose a stretch of beach or river and see just how much you can find in a set area. This is an activity which can take a while, or alternatively you could place a time limit of perhaps five minutes.

The longer a child looks, the more they are going to find. Look for unusual stones, starfish, seaweed, mermaid's purses (egg cases), sea wrack, sea glass, bones, shells, fossils, driftwood, different types of reeds, wading birds, ducks, and mud patterns.

Which are natural items and which are alien, eg: man made?

Is the river natural or man made? Remember that the canal network was purpose built to provide water transport across the UK. How can you tell it was man made? Look at structures, the line of the canal.

Walking in towns

Walking in towns need not just be an activity devoted to shopping. With a bit of thought and preparation, it is possible to have some really interesting town walks that can keep children occupied for some time. Talk to them about what they are seeing and what they should be looking out for, as well as dangers such as crossing the road or going under ladders. This will improve their road sense as well as their understanding of their environment. When children are interested and having fun, they do not realise how far they have walked.

Towns can be fascinating and intriguing places. There is always something happening and always something new to see. You do not have to just follow the main roads; you can explore side streets, alleys and squares. It is surprising what you can find when you start looking. Often these areas are much more interesting and offer a more varied scenery than main roads and shopping areas. Children are naturally curious and by encouraging them to explore, it will encourage them to see towns in a new light. It can also be safer – traffic tends to be lighter on less well-known streets. On sunny days, why not take some paper; pencils and something to lean on like a piece of cardboard or a book. Find a quiet corner perhaps in a square or alleyway that marks a convenient half way point or is just an interesting spot and let the children draw what they see – just like real artists.

Look out for unusual events such as sculpture trails that many towns hold throughout the year. This can provide an unusual talking point and an enjoyable activity for children as they hunt the sculpture. How many can they find?

Get a map of the town and plan your route in advance. Aim to go past places that will appeal to children. Younger children will enjoy going past the fire station or ambulance station. Will they be lucky enough to see vehicles going in or out? Perhaps the siren will be sounding? They might even see the engines being cleaned or the hosepipes rolled up. Encourage them to talk about what they are seeing and to make up stories about what the engines have been doing.

Alphabet

This is a simple word game that can be played as you walk. Can you find a building, place, vehicle or object to match every letter in the alphabet? The hardest way is to play this in purely alphabetical order only going on to the next letter once you have found a match for the previous one.

A simpler version is to write down all the alphabet letters on a pad before you leave. Then, when the game starts, write down matching words as they are seen. This is a much easier way for younger children to play Alphabet, as the pace of the game is faster.

Can you find?

Give children a challenge and they enjoy trying to beat you. This game is particularly suitable for older children. Time a walk through town to a chosen spot such as the Cathedral or a park. Can they find a shorter/longer route? Provide some maps and let them work out possible routes. Then, try out each route and work out which is the shortest, longest, prettiest or most interesting walk. Make sure the children lead the way, as it is the walk they have planned.

Possible variations could include:

Finding a route to a place they have never been to before.

Create timed walks; set a time limit for the duration of a walk such as half an hour, 45 minutes, one hour. The children have to create a walk that would last this amount of time. Only by actually walking it will they discover whether they are right or not.

This exercise encourages children to learn to read maps and find their own way around a town. It helps develop confidence, and makes them look closely at the route they are walking.

Counting games

Count the number of red cars, blue vans, dress shops, food shops.

Vehicles used by different type of traders, eg: plumbers, service engineers, shop vans, vehicle recovery, roadside assistance.

Older children, especially boys, could try counting specific types of cars such as Renault, Vauxhall, Ford, count the number of unusual vehicles or try to find one vehicle representing each type of manufacturer during the walk.

Finding games

Take: A pre-prepared list

Finding games are easy to create and give a lot of fun and interest to the walk. Such games encourage them to look closely at their environment and where they are walking. The game can be tailored to suit the ages of the children, with more complex lists provided for older children.

Preparation is essential. You need to know roughly where you are going to walk, and what you are likely to see. Decide in advance what has to be found by creating a list of places or things such as a fire engine, a church, a cathedral, a mosque, a thatched house, a specific street name, a pub sign, a blue bus. Make it a realistic list so that they have a chance of finding everything, but ensure that some cannot be found until towards the end of the walk.

Depending on the length of the walk, around 6 to 12 items should be included on the list. It can be a joint effort by all children present, or they can be competitive. Who will be the first to spot the cathedral? Who will be the first to find everything on the list?

You can try creating themes such as focusing on religious buildings, historic buildings, street names, and statues. Car mad children could be given the task of looking for a car made by each car manufacturer, or a specific range of cars. An alternative would be look for as many trades vehicles as they can; or to find as many flat roofed buildings, or lamp posts with a crest on them.

Ghost walks

Ghostly fox

These are a very popular walking activity in towns and have great appeal to older children. Taking place in the evening usually as dusk falls, it can be very atmospheric. When taking part in a ghost walk in York, we were greeted by a Victorian suited gentleman tolling a bell. All kinds of grisly, macabre and ghostly tales are told at selected locations along the route. In general such walks last between one to two hours and can cover several miles. Children are so interested, they do not realise how far they have walked. It offers an insight into an intriguing history of the town.

Such walks are not really suitable for very young children as the tales can be quite frightening and may result in nightmares!

High and low

Some preparation is needed but children can find this great fun to try to organise and take part in. Few towns and cities are built totally flat. Streets can wend their way up and down hills. Try to devise a walk that takes in as many high and low points as possible. Can the children work out whether they are actually walking high or low?

An alternative to this game would be to search out as many High Streets and Low Streets, or High Road and Low Road and find out if they really are.

How many?

This is a popular counting game that can be undertaken as you walk. There are many variations. You can create a theme or specify a number such as six churches to find from the beginning or a walk, or make it up as you go along. Typical suggestions could include:

> How many statues?
> How many statues of people?
> How many churches?
> How many gardens with hedges?
> How many blue cars?
> How many buses?
> How many Christmas decorations on the outside of houses?
> How many different types of buildings?

The list is endless. It encourages children to count, thus helping them learn their numbers. In addition, they learn to be observant, looking closely at the places through which they are walking. The game can be brought to an end quickly if they start to get tired or bored by it.

A competitive element can be introduced if more than one child is involved. Who can find the most churches or blue cars? Who will be the first to spot three statues? But be warned – you may need to act as a referee!

History walks

Most towns and cities have guides that lead historical walks. These are particularly suitable for children aged eight and upwards who like learning something about their environment. On a guided historical walk, the guide takes the group from place to place. At each stop along the walk, the guide tells a story or provides information about something that is related to the particular spot. Often these walks make you look at your town in a very new light, seeing buildings, monuments and even streets with

Roman legionary

a much wider knowledge. There may be tales of local people, of hidden rivers underneath your feet, about buildings which used to exist, houses with hidden stocks of gunpowder which exploded blowing out the windows of nearby churches. These are stories that bring history as well as your town to life in a very unforgettable way. The subject matter of the walks depends very much on the local area – it may be smugglers, dockyard tales, churches and castles, battles, Romans or Georgians. The guides are always very informative and keen to share their knowledge of local history.

Motifs

Look at buildings closely. Many will have various motifs on them. There could be shields, animals, pictures, logos, flowers or, criss cross designs. In some areas of the country, such as Suffolk, there is a long tradition of covering houses in decorative plasterwork known as pargeting. This can involve extremely complex designs.

Younger children could try and see how many motifs they can find and how many they recognise. Older children could do some art work by sketching interesting motifs and turning them into pictures when they return home.

Motifs

New places

Try and explore a different part of the town on each walk, so that the route is never the same. Move away from the main streets and look for little alleyways or corners to explore. Often the type of buildings to be found in such places is very different to the serried ranks of high street shop fronts. They can have a different atmosphere –

perhaps more closely built; they may be darker and more atmospheric, or might have unusual buildings.

Paving stone jump

A game that can be played wherever paving stones can be found. It can be played quite happily as you walk along. The aim is to jump over every second paving stone, landing safely on the third one. Pretend the alternate paving stones are islands surrounded by sharks. If you land on the wrong one, you might get caught.

Sometimes paving stones appear in different colours – choose a colour to jump over.

Pick a building

While walking, pick a building that can be seen some way ahead. Choose a building that stands out – it might have an unusual shape, be an unusual colour, or just be very prominent. Try and make up a quick story about it. Who works or lives in it? Is it a happy or sad place? What sort of story does it suggest? Magical, mysterious, frightening or silly?

It could either be played with one person making up the story; or as a round with each person saying a sentence that takes the story into a new direction.

Pub signs

Public houses can be found in all built up areas. They are always characterised by unusual names and decorative pub signs. Some are very historic such as the Kings Head, the Duke of Wellington or they can be quirky such as The Rat catcher, or The Mischief. How many different names can be found? What is the most unusual name? Is the pub sign a good depiction of the name or could the children do better? What stories can

The Dove

be made around the various pub signs? Prompt children by asking questions like who do you think was the Rat Catcher? When did he live? Would it be a fun job? What would happen if the rats caught him?

Looking at signs like this makes children more observant about their surroundings as well as stimulating their imagination.

Shapes

This is a game that can be played while walking. How many shapes can you find? A tree might be circular with a rectangular trunk, while a road could be a straight line. Do streets go off at right angles? Are there curves? Does the road lead you in a big circle or semicircle? How many squares can be seen? This can get competitive as children try to outdo each other. Referees are usually needed!

Shop signs

Traditionally, shops were recognised by a special symbol hung outside for example a barber's shop had a red and white pole. Such signs can still be found in old, historic cities and towns. How many can the children find while walking? Can they work out the meanings behind the signs – or can they make up possible reasons for the signs?

Statues

Towns and cities are full of statues to kings and queens, warriors, animals or mythological creatures. They are usually to be found in prominent places such as squares, outside churches or public buildings. Statues can even be found in more unusual locations like roofs, beside doors or in arches. There are several games that can be played.

How many statues can you find? This is a counting game that can get quite competitive. With some knowledge of the area, you could make it more detailed seeking just one type of statue like soldiers, animals or kings.

How many can you identify? This is harder and more suited to older children. Can they name the statue before reading its given name? Are there any stories about it?

Be a statue. As you pass each statue, children have to try to copy the position of the statue and see how long they can keep that position!

What would happen if the statue came to life? What would it do? What stories could it tell? This is an opportunity to make up stories about the statue. Each person could contribute a different story or you could make up a joint story with each child adding two or three sentences.

Street names

All roads and streets are named. There is always a story or reason behind the name. It might be obvious – Church Street in a street where there is a church; Dock Road leading to the docks, Bishop's Bridge near to a Bishop's house or more obscure such as Joy Road, Barrow Avenue, Haven Street, Mitre Road. Try and work out reasons for the road being given a name. There can be many possible reasons – a street can reflect its location, be named after someone famous or a local celebrity, after an event such as a battle, or after a group of people who used to carry on a trade in an area. Butchers Row in an old town would be where butchers used to have their shops while Heath Farm Road in a newly built up area might be so named because there used to be a farm bearing that name. Moor road could be a road leading to the moors; Queens drive might relate to a visit by the Queen or have been developed at a time when a Queen was being crowned or it could even have been a place where queens once drove in carriages!

Children enjoy making up stories behind the names. It spurs their imagination. You could try making up stories which could well have been possible, or make them funny, part of a mystery or even just devising the most silly reasons for a street being given a particular nam,e for example Bathhurst Close where a man named Mr Hurst used to have an bath.

An advantage to this game is that it encourages children to develop their vocabulary since street names often include unusual words like mitre or haberdasher, forge and yew tree. Geographical knowledge can also be helped since the street names may refer to places further away, for example Newmarket Road which is the road leading to the town of Newmarket.

Surface rubbings

Take: Paper, wax crayon or charcoal

Encourage kids to look closely at the surfaces of walls, buildings and trees that they pass. All have very different textures. There can even be decorative surfaces. Choose surfaces which are not too rough, and do not have any pieces sticking out that could pierce the paper. Put the paper on top of the surface and gently rub over with a wax crayon. It will leave an impression of the pattern and texture of the brick or stone underneath. As children become more skilled at this, they can use one sheet of paper to show the effect of different surfaces compared to each other, by using part of the paper for each surface. At home, these could be cut up and turned into unusual collages of people and buildings.

House date

Themed walks

This is an ideal activity for older children who enjoy a challenge and have some skill in map reading. Give them a theme such as churches, alleys, different types of architecture, public buildings. Their task is to plan a walk that will take them past say twelve churches, down 12 alleys or past all the public buildings in a town. Once planned, it has to be carried out just to make sure they are right. Leave it to the children to guide you on the walk.

This encourages them to use a map to plan and then follow the outlined route as they walk. It also encourages them to look closely at their locality and work out where there are places of interest.

Uniform search

When walking along streets in towns and cities, look out for people in uniform. How many can the children find? Can they identify their jobs? There could be policemen, firemen, soldiers, airmen, nurses, security guards, shop staf or, doormen outside big hotels.

Upwards and outwards

Encourage children to look upwards, not just at what they can see on the ground or at eye level. Surprises can be found. Shops may have modern fronts but when you look upwards you can see evidence of much older periods. Windows may be a very different design. There may be elaborate brick patterns involving different coloured bricks in arches or squares. Buildings may have dates built into the walls. Who can be the first to spot something unusual? What's the earliest date to be found?